IT'S ALL IN THE FACE

The FACTS and FANTASIES of FACE READING

Naomi R. Tickle

Daniels Publishing, Mountain View, California

IT'S ALL IN THE FACE

The FACTS and FANTASIES of FACE READING

Naomi R. Tickle

Published by: Daniels Publishing
Post Office Box 4439
Mountain View, California 94040, USA

Copyright © 1995 by Naomi R. Tickle
First Printing 1995
Library of Congress Catalog Card Number 95-069011

ISBN 0-9646398-0-7

Printed in the United States
10 9 8 7 6 5 4 3 2 1

Photographs of Celebrities by Shooting Stars International
Book cover illustration by Tana Powell, San Francisco
Book cover design by Karen Monroe of Monroe Graphics
Inside illustrations by Edward Fowler

ACKNOWLEDGEMENTS

This book would not have been possible without the opportunity to meet and study with some of the people responsible for the development of Personology. Robert Whiteside, pioneer and founder of Personology, and William Burtis who, along with several other dedicated personologists, were responsible for the science known today as Personology. The late Suzanne Caygill (founder of color analysis in 1945) whose work inspired me to seek further a greater understanding of the patterns and designs seen in the human being. To my husband Andrew for his incredible patience and support for my work over the past 15 years. To my friends Cindi Lynch, Lorraine Kamisky and Stephen Fairchild whose contribution and continued support has been greatly appreciated. Thanks are due to Bruce Vaughan for his insight on jury selection, and to Don Wilson (who has used personology for over fourty years) for his encouragement and enthusiasm.

About the Author

Naomi Tickle is a Certified Personologist and Instructor from the Personology Institute. Her interest in personology, the relationship between facial features and personality, began fifteen years ago when she was studying at the Academy of Color in San Francisco. The unique approach to colour, taught by the academy, revealed how certain groups of colours harmonized best with the eye, hair and skin pigmentation, and these groups were the basis of the most flattering colours and combinations to wear.

Through her work with thousands of clients, Naomi found that these colour groups also told much about people, such as their preferences for antique or modern decor, geometric or flowing patterns, and their preferred geographical environment. In fact her continued research with clients suggested a probable genetic limk between colour groups and innate preferences.

Naomi has taken her work in relating physical characteristics to psychological characteristics a step further in this treatise on personology. Through this practice Naomi helps others get in touch with their inner qualities and abilities to bring balance and harmony into their lives, whether they are looking for the career that most follows their heart's desire, or seeking a deeper understanding of themselves.

Personology provides an approach to discovering a part of the human puzzle. Every person has a sense of what "feels right" or "rings true" for him or her, even though it may not be "known" at a concious level. Personology unveils or confirms these "truths" about an individual, giving each a sense of personal validation and "permission" to move forward in his or her life.

FOREWORD

Personology relates the human physical structure to the native behavioral functioning process. The premise and major theme of personology is that structure pre-disposes or inclines function, but *freedom of choice* can overcome structure.

Over the years, growing attention has been focused on the relationship between physical structure in humans and their behaviour. There is now known to be a correlation between personology and the basic sciences of physiology, anatomy and neurology. The science of genetics also plays a role in the study of personological factors and traits.

Today, teachers and counselors in the field of personology are able to provide their students and clientele with specific, down-to-earth information and recommendations on better understanding of their own make-up, relating more effectively to family members, improving human relations on the job or in the political arena and selecting the right career.

Personology helps people to take a more practical approach to all aspects of daily living.

William F. Burtis, M.S. Personologist

TABLE OF CONTENTS

LET'S FACE IT

We all read faces, we can't avoid it. It's both an ancient art and a modern science. Some get more useful information from it than others. In the pace of business activities and personal life, we are constantly meeting new people and reaffirming our relationships and expectations of those familiar to us. There is seldom time to get to know and understand them before important decisions have to be made, agreements reached and new acquaintances either remembered or forgotten.

It is always easier to deal with people and faces we know. This is why in business, as long as there are no problems, we tend to keep the same suppliers and customers and get to know them better. We also tend to keep the same friends, doctors, dentists, plumbers and family photographers.

Today, many corporations recognize the need for people to understand each other better before they can work together effectively. To this end they have used written tests to categorize psychological and personality traits. Workshops have also been used successfully, where groups study each other's behaviour and then label it as the majority perceive it. Some participants later use small placards on their desks to announce to their peers such personal styles as *expressive amiable, analytical driver, etc.* This may seem extreme to anyone who has not been involved in the process. However it does show the importance people attach to understanding each other quickly before working together. This is fine for corporations, however the rest of us need something which gives similiar results without written tests or lengthy behaviour study. Many professions now recognize that face reading can

It's All in the Face

provide critical information quickly.

Commonly used expressions such as *nose for news, highbrow, tight lipped* and *conehead* show that we associate facial features with behaviour. Cartoonists and casting directors for film and theatre strive to select faces that convince us of the characters portrayed.

The relationship of facial structure to the personality within has intrigued and puzzled scientists since early times. The serious study of faces, and their relationship to the personality within, originated independently in China, and in Greece with ancient Greeks such as Pythagoras (of triangle fame) and Aristotle. In the Roman Empire it became a respected profession, and in England during the reign of Elizabeth the First it was considered a threat to the authorities, and was punishable by whipping. In the twentieth century three men changed it into a modern science. Edward Vincent Jones, a California judge, categorically linked facial features and character traits. Robert Whiteside worked on statistically validating these linkages, and was subsequently joined by William Burtis. They continued the testing and correlation of over seventy facial features and behaviour traits.

In activities as diverse as jury selection, selling face to face, and resolving family problems, faces are spelling out vital information. This book is an illustrated guide designed to help you recognize facial features that indicate how people will react.

HISTORICAL BACKGROUND
OF PERSONOLOGY

When early man gazed on the ferocious face of the crocodile he must have been struck by the relationship between appearance and behaviour. We might have expected that this would have been extended in more detailed and subtle ways to the study of his fellow men. We might expect that this study would have developed into a science of its own, at least as old as the written word itself. In fact this did not happen until the twentieth century.

Why so many centuries of delay?

One investigator of appearance and behaviour was the Greek philosopher Pythagoras in the sixth century BC. His concern was the "soul" of man, and today we have to recognize that was a far tougher project than his geometry theorems. A couple of centuries later, in the fourth century BC, Aristotle came up with the intriguing notion of understanding man's character by comparing his qualities and appearance with similar qualities and appearances in animals. Eventually the interest in Greece and Europe moved toward practical understanding of people.

As time passed through the Dark Ages and the Middle Ages, interest in the appearance-behaviour concept came and went. It was tied in with astrological divinations and then forgotten, and never got established on its own. We have to remember that in those days things were very different from today.

In those far off days there was not a scientific method, nor a scientific culture as we know it today. It was more of a mind game. The philosophers dealt much more in ideas (theory) than they did in actual information (data). If an idea was sufficiently brilliant or appealing it might be accepted without today's burden of proof. However if attempts were made to put the scheme to serious use before proper (modern) testing, then results could be unpredictable.

There was often a real barrier to new knowledge and ideas, however important, when they contradicted or competed with established doctrines and politics. Remember the opposition to abandoning the flat earth in favor of the round one, and having the planets orbit the sun instead of the earth? Then there was the case of a man arrested for fraud, when he claimed he could transmit voice by wire.

So without the scientific muscle and will, it is not surprising looking back that any use was made of the appearance-behaviour concept until the present century. The old world simply was not ready for it.

What emerged throughout Europe during the Age of Enlightenment and into the early part of the nineteenth century, was a common theory that certain human body shapes had an effect on human behaviour. A trio of German doctors - Lavater, Gall and Spurzheim- developed a comprehensive thesis based on this supposition.

From these well-known scientists' works a surge of popularity was spawned for phrenology (the study of the shape of the human skull and its relationship to human personality) throughout Germany, Austria and France at the turn of the twentieth century. Even the European medical community seriously explored phrenology and conducted extensive research into the relationship between phrenology, biochemistry, and the genetic make up of an individual.

It was during this time that the American George Fowler brought these studies and the various findings on phrenology to the

United States. He became a noted phrenologist in his own right as well as a New York society darling until he and his work fell into disrepute.

While that phrenology was gaining popular attention in Europe and Fowler was enjoying success in the U.S., the philosopher Hans Christian Smutz emerged as Prime Minister of South Africa. His compelling interest into the relationship between ethnic and genetic origins led him to coin the term personology.

It was Edward Vincent Jones, a California judge, who put the subject on a modern footing. He wanted to know if certain behaviour traits correlated with physical features.

Judge Jones had many opportunities to study the physical features and the behaviour of defendants, witnesses and attorneys for the prosecution and the defense. He recorded facial features and the characteristics that accompanied them. As the amount of data accumulated, Jones saw that there were clear-cut trends. At this point Jones met Robert Whiteside, whose interest matched his own intensity for the subject.

Robert Whiteside continued their research and termed it personology - literally the study of persons - and supplied the statistical testing and validation. The system was further developed to use detailed measurements of over one hundred traits.

CONCEPTS

Personology gives us a "blue print" to better understand ourselves and how we can improve our communications with others, bringing balance and harmony into our lives

CONCEPTS

Faces and Behaviour

The behaviour traits described in this book, and the facial features that predict them, were discovered purely by repeated observation by Edward Vincent Jones during thousands of courtroom cases, and later validated by Robert Whiteside [Reference 1], and William Burtis. Robert Whiteside subsequently directed in 1950 a study of 1050 adults from California and Oregon. Measurements of sixty-seven facial features were recorded and correlated with personality factors using standard statistical techniques. The analysis of the results showed an impressive 92% accuracy-per-trait.

A later survey of a group of 492 individuals showed that vocational recommendations based on facial analysis worked out at 96% self professed job satisfaction. When personology was used in the marriage the information elicited helped couples in 92% of the cases.

Face reading is based on facts. Although some publishers and bookstores place it in the supernatural category, it has no relation to mysticism, spirituality or altered states of consciousness. However people skilled in these areas will appreciate the insights which can be gained from reading faces.

Since there is no underlying theory or explanation to grasp, face reading is a very simple and uncomplicated exercise. What you see is what you get!

Disclaimers

In the past, reading faces has been associated with fields as widely divergent as astrology and structural genetics. It is important here to state some disclaimers.

Face reading, as described in this book, is not involved with genetics since we are not concerned with characteristics of the parents, only the individual. Neither are we concerned how a trait was inherited (i.e., from the mother's or father's side of the family), nor are we concerned with which genes control it.

The innate abilities and characteristics we inherit are only one of the forces controlling our lives. Early nurturing and the experiences of childhood (and later) strongly shape the growth of our personalities. Of course, after childhood we can still, by conscious desire and choice, change our attitudes, behaviour and activities.

We assert only that we are born with certain easily recognizable features in the face which become clearly discernable during childhood and then remain for life; and that these features accurately predict behaviour and personality traits.

Enhancing Your Perception
Whenever we see a new face, we are instinctively aware of the gender and age, which we record with no conscious effort. The facial features spell out information on character traits that we can learn to read and interpret as automatically as we read sex and age. As we learn to recognize new facial features, and become confident of the traits they predict, this becomes a part of our immediate perception. With these skills, when we meet new people, we already know many things about them before a single word has been spoken.

Trait Combinations
A behaviour trait on its own may not be that significant, particularly if it is not a strong one. However if this trait occurs in combination with other traits, the effect may be strongly modified or reinforced.

It's All in the Face

Asymmetrical Faces - Mood swings

The stronger the differences between the two sides of the face, the greater are the mood swings. This is the result of the parents being significantly different from each other in their appearance. The child inherits physical features from each parent. Some people may feel they have dual personalities because of the push and pull of the different traits. For example, one moment a person may be very tolerant and the next very intolerant. The person has no idea when the mood will change. Once people with these strong mood swings realize a possible cause for them, they are able to exert more control.

Instinctive Behaviour and Learned Behaviour

The fact that a person has low innate self-confidence does not imply a value judgement, nor does it imply a difficulty coping with life. First let's look at how we understand the word *self-confidence*. We all agree that it is good to have self-confidence. We like to have it in ourselves and to see it in others. It gives us the reassuring feeling that people know what they are doing. Self-confidence may be innate (inherited) or learned.

The way people handle new situations is revealing about Self-confidence. An innately self-confident person will welcome new situations and will handle any problems that occur on the fly. People with lower self-confidence do not look forward to surprises, and will worry about the problems that might occur. Their concern can drive them to understand everything possible ahead of time, and to talk to others whose experience would be helpful, and generally be as informed and prepared as possible ahead of time. This thorough preparation can make them successful and becomes a learned behaviour pattern. People with innately high or innately low self-confidence will both be successful, but use different approaches.

Conscious Choice

Because we have inherited traits, which stay with us for life, it does not mean we do not have control over our behaviour or the way in which those traits are expressed. Once those traits which have a significant impact on the way we behave or communicate are identified, we can consciously choose to suppress a basic urge when it is not appropriate. Take for example someone who has a high temper, is extremely physical, forceful and ruthlless. This person might be inclined towards violence. However, once the individual is aware of his innate characteristics, he can choose to gain control of these traits and use their energy in a more productive and supportive way. In fact, these types of people can learn to avoid or remove themselves from situations which stimulate negative actions. Another example would be someone who is always late for appointments. This would indicate high tolerance. People with this trait can discipline themselves to arrive on time once they know this is part of their inherent nature. The choice is ultimately each individual's decision and responsibility.

Our Mixed Heritage

The different species of birds build their nests with distinct shapes. The robin, swallow and eagle will each stay with their own unchanging style of nest year after year, and generation after generation. The fixed patterns and preferred environments are so important that migratory birds travel thousands of miles to nest in a specific place. When the human race spread throughout the world it adapted, like the wild life, to each region and its environment. However, unlike wildlife, there are now very few regions of the earth where racial "purity" still exists, since racial characteristics are no longer vital to surviving the local conditions. Mankind has now emerged with complex patterns resulting from its mixed heritage. Today, humans live in surroundings that may be quite different from their inherited mixtures of natural habitats and environmental preferences.

By the ocean or in the mountains? Town or country living? Architectural style? Elegant or textured surfaces and furnishings? Geometric or flowing designs? We look at the choices and say we prefer this rather than that, not realizing we are expressing our own innate preferences. If you are unsure of this, then take a look at the shapes, colours and textures and activities that you consistently select. When these are selected without regard to fashion, habit or cost, they reflect innate patterns of preferences.

By understanding and identifying our innate patterns, there is a strong sense of self-validation. There is also a feeling of being more centered, and less influenced by commercial pressures telling us what we should buy and how we should spend our time.

There is a resonance that we feel, when surrounded by the colours, designs and environment we enjoy. We feel "in tune" with our lives, with a piece of music we listen to, being by the water or walking through the woods, playing tennis or shooting the rapids.

Self-Knowledge

The quest for self-knowledge, which was once regarded as fanciful introspection, has progressed to bookshelves dedicated to self-understanding, self-awareness, self-discipline, self-education, self-improvement etc. The ideas expounded vary greatly on each author's view about what you are born with, what you grew up with and what to do about it. Face reading provides a good starting point for understanding what traits we inherited at birth.

In short, understanding personality traits is useful to anyone who deals with other people (and who doesn't?). But despite the many practical business applications of personology, this book is also intended for the individual to use as a practical guide in everyday life. Understanding your own traits is a critical first step towards becoming the individual you want to be.

This book does not claim that personology performs miracles, nor does it claim that a reader will magically transform into a healthy, fulfilled human being. What it can do is to provide an introductory map to assist a reader on his or her personal quest -- not for ultimate answers -- but toward an inner understanding of oneself and learning how to communicate with others more effectively. Personology allows us a glimpse at the possibilities on how to get in touch with who we are, rather than buying into a commercial image. Men, unlike women, haven't usually allowed themselves the opportunity to explore their inner selves. They have been caught up in performing what is expected of them.

Consultations

Personology consultations based on detailed face reading are available throughout the United States and Europe. These offer the client significantly more information than the scope of this book. The accuracy of measurement is much more precise since personologists use standard procedures and special tools. In this book a facial feature is considered either significant, or it is ignored. The personologist however, after completing the measurements, will categorize a trait as high, average or low. After the results have been calculated from the measurements, they are then documented as a permanent record on a chart.

Another service usually included in a consultation is career matching. A computer is used to search for careers which best match the client's innate abilities and traits. This service has nothing to do with salaries, availability of jobs or the client's experience. The major benefit is that it is based only on innate abilities, and is therefore valuable when clarifying new career directions. In the initial 1960 survey on vocational recommendations, it was found that the jobs selected for the individual worked out to 96% accuracy, as indicated by self-proclaimed job satisfaction.

Even when a client is not currently interested in a new career, the results are fascinating and explain the yearnings and fantasies of earlier years.

Besides the fifty-two traits described in this book, there are over forty additional traits measured during a consultation that are not described here. These additional traits are also key indicators for career matching.

The last benefit of a consultation, of course, is objectivity. No matter how skilled you become, it is hard to be objective about yourself. We try to be fair to ourselves, but usually we are somewhere between trying not to flatter ourselves and trying not to be too hard on ourselves. The personologist has neither motivation, and can therefore provide an unbiased perspective.

Organization of the Book

The traits described in this book are grouped loosely into four areas, which are described in the next four Chapters.

Physical Traits	are associated with physical situations such as whether a person is built physically to sit or stand for long periods of time.
Automatic Expression	traits are more spontaneous, e.g., Emotional Expressiveness and Impulsiveness.
Feelings and Emotions	involve feelings such as Self-Confidence and Tolerance.
Thinking Traits	involve the way we process information, e.g. the need to analyse and critique it, to review it step by step or race to conclusions.

By examining each of these four areas, a primary personality comes into focus. The traits by themselves predict behavioural pattern. However, when combined with other traits, the effects may be modified or reinforced. The combination gives people a better perspective of themselves and others. Instead of people being regarded as strange and not fitting the norm (whatever that may be), we find the behaviour that is normal for them and it's really o.k.

As you read these chapters and begin to focus on single traits in isolation, it is important to keep in mind that each individual trait must be seen in context with other characteristics as well as the whole individual -- a person's overall style, approach to life, and basic motivations. There is much more work to be done in the field of linking the structure/function relationship. The traits included in this book have been tested out on thousands of people and found to be 92 percent accurate. Once you have mastered some of these traits, you may notice others which have not been mentioned in this book. Remember it takes a large number of observations for new information to be validated.

We will now explore some of these concepts. It will be easier to practice your new found knowledge on others, since it is harder to be objective about oneself. You might want to begin with photographs of family and friends.

PHYSICAL TRAITS

- **Foot Dexterity**
- **Hand Dexterity**
- **Risk Taking**
- **Philosophical Trend**
- **Physical Insulation**
- **Serious Mindedness**
- **Physicalness**

FOOT DEXTERITY

This is not skill in kicking field goals, but the measurement of how long the legs are in proportion to the body. This basic ratio determines where the center of gravity is, and whether a person is built to sit or stand comfortably most of the time.

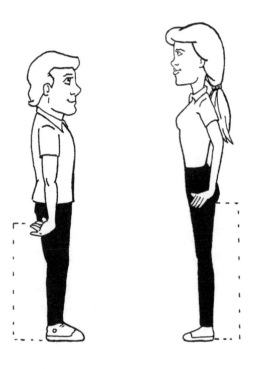

Fig. 1   High Foot Dexterity   *Low Foot Dexterity*

Low Foot Dexterity

People with short torsos and long legs (high center of gravity) do their best thinking and working in a sitting position, such as desk jobs or any activity that takes them off their feet. They are not built to be on their legs for long periods of time. Should they

27

do so they may develop back problems. If they are in a situation where standing for a length of time is necessary, they need to take a break and sit down to avoid back stress and irritation.

Recommended sports activities could be basketball, kyaking, swimming, tai-chi, ice skating. Related careers would include computer programming, accounting, sewing, receptionist, truck or taxi cab driver.

High Foot Dexterity

People built with a long torso and short legs (low center of gravity) will have an easier time standing and working on their feet. Sitting for long periods of time makes them restless, and this will have a direct bearing on vocational selection and basic physical needs. Physical activities would include hiking, jogging, running, tennis, soccer, football, gardening, aerobics, wrestling, mountain climbing. Related careers would include (depending of course on the other traits) sales, construction, architecture, beautician, nursing, gardening, military officer.

A person who is neither long nor short legged will be adaptable, and will not spend long periods of time either sitting or standing. Sports and careers should be a balanced combination of both.

Directing High Foot Dexterity

When you are feeling restless, take a walk or get some physical exercise. This will help you maintain a balance through the day. Exercise is a good activity for solving problems or mood shifts.

Learn to recognize this trait in others. If you are vacationing with friends who are on the opposite pole, understand they will need rest periods between activities. Or if you are in a situation where there are long periods of being on the feet, suggest a coffee break. Your time will be more productive.

Directing Low Foot Dexterity
Select a career which allows you to be off your feet. If you are in a job that requires standing all day, make sure you take short rest periods. If possible, find a seat and rest the legs. When on a vacation, plan a mixture of touring and physical activity. Make sure your travel companions are of similar build. If not, work something out ahead of time so that the activities are compatible with both parties.

HAND DEXTERITY

Manual dexterity is found by the evenness of the lengths of the three middle fingers. People with fingers close in length have more innate skill when working with their hands, since they can grasp and manipulate objects more effectively. People who do not have this trait have to work harder to achieve the same results. This explains why some people love to work with their hands while others never show any interest.

Spatulation is a flattening of the ends of the fingers. If fingers are spatulated, the ability to work with fine craftsmanship is enhanced. This is often caused by working constantly with the hands, such as in sculpture, pottery, gardening, dental or mechanical work.

When a person has low Hand Dexterity, (high variation in length of three middle fingers) other traits may augment or modify this activity such as Carefulness, Concentration and Exactingness.

Directing High Hand Dexterity
People with high Hand Dexterity have a natural ability to work with their hands. It takes less effort for them to get good results. Use this ability for either a hobby or as a vocation.

Vocations where this trait could be used are massage therapist, chiropractor, physical therapy, dentistry, hair design (with high design appreciation) carpentry, art and crafts, fine jeweler or musician.

Fig. 2   Low Hand Dexterity   *High Hand Dexterity*

Directing Low Hand Dexterity

In order for people with low Hand Dexterity to achieve the same results, they will need to concentrate more on what they are doing. These people will find themselves working harder to achieve the same results as those with natural dexterity. If you are involved with hobbies or other activities where hand coordination is needed, allow yourself more time.

RISK TAKING

Risk taking correlates with the length of the ring finger compared with the index finger. This is best viewed with the palm of the hand facing you. If the ring finger is longer this indicates someone who is comfortable taking a risk. When there is a difference between the two hands in the finger measurement, this indicates someone comfortable taking risks and at other times being more conservative. When the ring finger is shorter than the index finger this indicates a more cautious nature, and if risks are taken they are calculated risks.

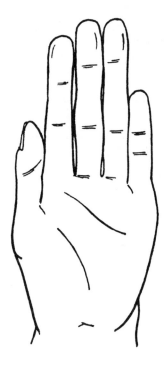

Figure 3   Risk Taking

31

It's All in the Face

High Risk

A risk could be anything from adrenaline releasing physical activities like skydiving, to more intellectual and passive ventures such as speculating in the stock market. People who score high on this trait enjoy the thrill that comes with taking chances. Sometimes they are willing to risk all, without considering the consequences.

Low Risk Taking

When people are more conservative, the risks, in general, are more calculated. They will consider all aspects of the situation before taking a chance. They will put their investments into a secure market. Sometimes this conservative approach can hold people back from achieving their goals or changing career directions. A risk for these people could be changing jobs, living in a new city or participating in a new activity. This may appear dull to those people who are natural risk takers. However, low risk takers are operating out of their own comfort zone. Risk taking is on a different level for them.

Directing Low Risk Taking

If you are very conservative, experience taking a risk now and again, it will help to stretch your perceived limitations. If there is some element of risk, familiarize yourself with what it entails. You will then be able to approach the situation with more confidence. Don't dampen the enthusiasm of people who are seekers of the unknown.

How to Direct High Risk Taking

Consider how the risk could effect other people's lives. Participate in a sport or other activities which satisfy the need to take chances. Do not expect low risk takers to eagerly embrace your passion for risk.

PHILOSOPHICAL TREND

This trait was first identified by the Egyptians 3000 BC. It was observed that there was a strong correlation between the gaps in the fingers and philosophical tendencies. When the palms are viewed with the fingers together against the light, there is a certain amount of space visible between the fingers where the light shines through.

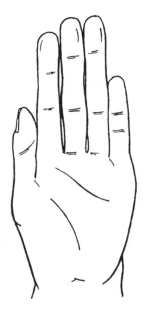 

Fig. 4   *Low Philosophical Trend*   *High Philosophical Trend*

Significant gaps show a more philosophical person who may look for a deeper meaning in life. When there is no gaping between the fingers, this shows there is little or no interest in philosophical tendencies. People with a strong Philosophical Trend are continually searching for answers, and are restless until they get a sense of their own balance and harmony. They have an innate sense for spiritual values and seek a purpose beyond material levels. These people may go on a lifelong personal quest to seek a lifestyle that gives them a deeper meaning and satisfaction. There is an inner awareness that seeks tranquility. They need to get in touch with themselves on a spiritual level. They may go on retreats or travel to India to study under a guru to find their answers and to get in touch with their spiritual needs. Avocations include the pursuit of evangelistic and philosophical issues and metaphysics. Occupations would include the ministry, leading philosophical workshops and seminars.

Directing a Philosophical Trend

Attend, or offer, workshops on philosophical, spiritual or religious interests. Learn to keep personal beliefs in perspective. Be willing to listen and understand other people's viewpoints on philosophical or religious discussions.

PHYSICAL INSULATION

Physical Insulation measures a person's insulation to external circumstances such as sound, touch, taste, feelings and environment. This measurement is taken from the thickness of a hair follicle (a single strand of hair).

Low Physical Insulation

The finer the hair the more sensitive the person is to smell, sound, taste, elegance versus roughness. Individuals with fine hair prefer quality rather than quantity. Their feelings get hurt very quickly, and they are much quicker to react to "outside" influences. Camping out in the rough is not as enjoyable as staying in a bed and breakfast for the night. They thrive in a more protective environment. If the camping situation has sufficient comforts then that might be more acceptable. They become quickly irritated when people around them are coarse or loud.

Fig. 5 High Physical Insulation   *Low Physical Insulation*

High Physical Insulation

People with thicker hair follicles need more stimulation to elicit a response. These people are less sensitive to pain.   They like things to be on a grand scale both in sound, amounts of food, laughter, the big beat of the drum and strong vibrant rhythms. They love the outdoors, camping and the extreme elements of the sun, wind, rain and snow. It takes longer to get under their skin, and they may appear insensitive to other people s needs. They are much more physical than emotional in expression and reaction.

People who have hair that is of medium thickness will find they are able to adapt easily to what is around them, they are more easily able to give and take. Just being more aware of others helps them know which way to interact with them.

Directing Low Physical Insulation

If you are have low Physical Insulation, recognize that you are very sensitive, and understand that others are not intending to hurt or offend you. When this trait is combined with high Emotionality and low Tolerance (Figure 31) you may over react. Consciously choose to be in control of your reactions. When other people seem loud or rough, notice whether the hair is coarse or if they have high tolerance and Self-Confidence (Figures 32 & 30). Understand why you are reacting to them. Either adjust your own reactions or remove yourself from that environment.

Directing High Physical Insulation

People with high Physical Insulation are less sensitive to the needs of others. For example when they are with people who have finer hair, they could be more popular by asking them if the music is too loud, or how can they make the camping experience more comfortable. If you have high Physical Insulation, be aware that others may be more sensitive, and modify your expression and actions. Use a softer tone, be considerate. Think in terms of quality, especially when giving gift. When you are with people who have similar traits, you can interact with them on the same level.

SERIOUS MINDEDNESS

Deep-set eyes show Serious Mindedness. People with this trait take life, work and responsibilities extremely seriously. They may not always see the more humorous side of life. When you give these people a job to do, it will be well done.

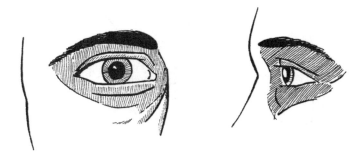

Figure 6   Serious Mindedness

Trait Combinations

The effect of Serious Mindedness will be amplified when combined with low Tolerance(Figure31) and fine hair. Those with this combination are inclined to be even more thoughtful and reflective. Small issues become more significant.

Directing Serious Mindedness

To create a more balanced life, Serious Minded people need to develop a lighter side and learn not to take life so seriously. They need to take up a hobby or physical activity which will help them to relax and have fun. Examples of this trait would be Cher, Nancy Reagan, Abraham Lincoln and Ghandi.

PHYSICALNESS

The bony protuberance at the back of the head (the cerebellum) indicates the need for physical activity. It also indicates how quickly a person is physically stimulated. This physical drive is expressed both mentally and through physical activity.

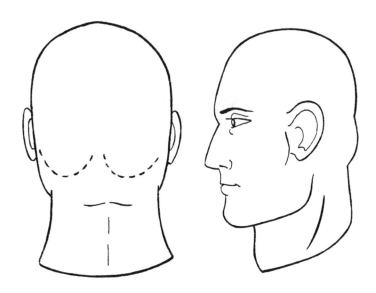

Fig. 8   High Physicalness

High Physicalness
Once people with this trait get an idea or goal, they want to immediately put it into action. These are the people who move the piano instead of the stool.   They enjoy physical activities, and exercise needs to be a part of their daily routine otherwise they become restless and irritable.

Low Physicalness

People who score low on Physicalness enjoy being spectators rather than being physically involved. To others they may appear to be lazy and boring, particularly when this trait is combined with long legs (Figure 1). People who score high on these two traits may be called "couch potatoes" when biologically they do not feel an urgent physical need for exercise. They're quite comfortable being at home, enjoying a good book or watching their favourite television programme. They do not have the same physical stamina or staying power as the people who are have a higher score on Physicalness. This could be a problem in a relationship if the other person is on the opposite pole. One would want to be active while the other is quite happy to sit in a chair.

Trait Combinations

This trait is amplified when combined with Physical Motive (Figure 40). People with both these traits are very enthusiastic people and pour energy into everything they do.

People with Physical Motive (Figure 40), Forcefulness and high Physicalness provide a driving force in getting projects started and completed. They want it done now. If their traits also include low Self-Confidence, then in the eagerness to get things finished, they may not do a thorough job. These are very intense people who find it hard to relax. They are much happier kept busy otherwise they become quickly bored. This is an advantage when there are projects waiting to be started.

Directing Low Physicalness

Make sure you take some time to exercise during the day. When with others who are more physical, make sure you've had plenty of rest the day before.

Directing High Physicalness

Take up hobbies that involve physical activity. Understand that not everyone likes to move at the same pace.

AUTOMATIC EXPRESSION TRAITS

- **Authoritative**
- **Self-Reliance**
- **Tenacity**
- **Pioneering Trend**
- **Adventurous**
- **Automatic Giving**
- **Pride in Personal Appearance**
- **Dry Wit**
- **Automatic Resistance**
- **Administrative/Ministrative**
- **Concise/Verbose**
- **Impulsive**
- **Credulity/Skepticism**

It's All in the Face

Successful communication is achieved
by understanding
people's feelings and emotions.

AUTHORITATIVE

The Authoritative trait is expressed physically by the width of the jaw line in comparison to the width of Self-Confidence line which is the width beween the vertical ridge found near the outside of the eye brow (Figures 29 and 30). When the jaw line is wider than the Self-Confidence line the Authoritativeness trait is high. As the jaw line becomes narrower than the Self-Confidence line, the Authoritative trait is less pronounced.

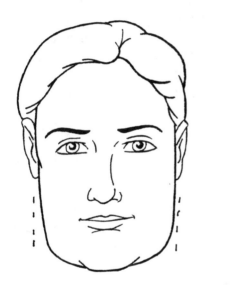

Fig. 9 High Authoritativeness   *Fig. 10 Low Authoritativeness*

The appearance of authority and of being in command of the situation is also enhanced by a wide jaw. The quality and tone of the voice add to the effect, so that a person both sounds and looks

It's All in the Face

in charge. These individuals have a commanding nature and sound very convincing.

People with width at the outer edge of the eye line (high Self-Confidence, Figure 30) and wide jaws appear powerful as distinct from merely authoritative. They are decisive, and do well both in communication and action. They gain respect from others, and because of their decisive tone, manner and total lack of doubt, they appear in command. Examples are General Swartzkopf, Churchill, Diane Feinstein, Barbara Bush, Margaret Thatcher and Bill Clinton.

People with this trait may be annoying to some because they appear as "know it all's" when the behaviour is not in check. They can quite unintentionally take over a conversation or discussion through their authoritativeness, although their intent was to draw it out. The appearance of too much authority can be intimidating, to others, causing concern or discomfort about expressing a different viewpoint or conflicting information. Authoritative figures need to consciously invite others to take the lead in discussion.

In a large aerospace company, employees were having a problem with their new boss. This person was very Authoritative, high Self-Confident and forceful. When she wore her bright red outfit, she was perceived as very aggressive. It was tactfully suggested that she should wear a softer colour at the next employee meeting, a colour that would subdue the natural authority she exuded rather than accentuate it. The results spoke for themselves. When people are physically Authoritative, they need to learn when stronger or softer colours are more appropriate.

The people who are low on the authoritative trait are indecisive or not very strong in their convictions. Their voices are softer and sound more diplomatic. They need to cultivate a tone of authoritativeness, act with definite intent. When low authority features are combined with fine hair, this person needs to raise the volume of the voice, deepen the tone, and use bigger gestures to give the appearance of authority. In a situation when a stronger statement will be needed, wearing deeper, stronger colours will support the position. Usually they are easy to talk to. They exchange ideas and information more readily, and treat each other as equals. Examples are Bill Clinton (high Authoritativeness) versus Johnny Carson (low Authoritativeness).

Trait Combinations

When other trait combinations are evident with low Authoritativeness such as Sharpness and Forcefulness, this overcomes the lack of authority to make the appearance more aggressive, for example Ross Perot, Marcia Clark (Prosecuting attorney for the O.J. Simpson trial).

Directing High Authoritativeness

Unless you are actually in authority, let others take the lead. Use a softer tone when needed. Wearing formal colours strengthens your authority, which may be intimidating. Using softer colours will open discussion, whether one on one, or in a group session.

When working with people who are both Authoritative and Forceful, do not try to force them to back down. Discuss the issue with them, use a more subtle approach by which their ego is not diminished.

Directing Low Authoritativeness

Cultivate a more definite tone of voice. Speak with confidence, let people know that you are knowledgeable. When you need more authority, wear more formal colours. Buy a pair of glasses (even if they are not needed), the frame adds strength to the facial design.

SELF-RELIANCE

This is found by how much the nostrils flare out from the nose. The greater the flare the higher is the Self-Reliance. People with high Self-Reliance know how to use their own inner resources to get things done or overcome adversity. If they were lost in the desert, they would have a strong sense that they would find their way out. Their inner conversation is "I know I can do it.". They instinctively know how to handle different situations.

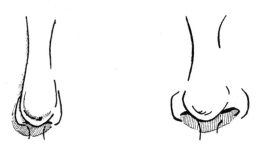

Fig.11   Low Self-Reliance   *Fig. 12   High Self-Reliance*

People with low Self-Reliance may be too dependent on others for decisions and direction. They do not always give themselves credit for what they know. Their inner conversation is one of questioning whether they will succeed. They do not welcome new situations, and recall all the times unfamiliar situations have worked against them. For example they may gather all the necessary information for starting a business or project, but then not follow through when a situation occurs that puts doubt in their minds.

Trait Combinations

When low Self-Reliance is combined with low Self-Confidence, these individuals may rely heavily on other people to handle projects. However they are more than willing to accept advice and follow directions.

Directing High Self-Reliance

People with high Self-Reliance are very independent and prefer to tackle a job their way rather than follow others. This may alienate them from the team. If you have high Self-Reliance, recognize when it can work for or against you.

Directing Low Self-Reliance

Learn to make your own decisions. Think things through before you get involved in new situations. Write out what steps need to be taken to achieve the best results. At the end, acknowledge your achievement. Note how much you have learned by relying on your own decisions, whether it was positive or negative. Before taking on a project, take a deep breath and tell yourself you can do it. Do not dwell on your past failures, this will inhibit your growth.

It's All in the Face

TENACITY

This is indicated by the amount of chin protruding forward when viewed from the side profile. The more it protrudes forward, the more Tenacious is the person. A receding chin indicates less Tenacity.

People with high Tenacity can tolerate difficult situations for a long time. Once they get their teeth into a project or relationship, they hang on till the bitter end. Examples are Robin Williams, Marlon Brando, and John Tesh.

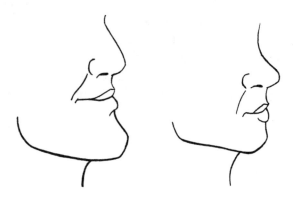

Figure. 13 High Tenacity (Protruding chin)
Low Tenacity (chin recedes)

Directing High Tenacity

If you are a person with high Tenacity, you may fail to recognize that what you are doing is no longer working. Know when it's time to let go rather than hanging on hoping things will work out, when realistically the odds are strongly against that happening. Hang on for the right reasons.

Directing Low Tenacity

People with less Tenacity will "let go" of a situation, when there is no advantage to "hanging on". They are however, more willing to find another way around the problem. An example is Prince Charles.

PIONEERING TREND

This trait is shown by the straightness of the outside rim (helix) of the ear. People with this trait have an entrepreneurial spirit. They like to explore new territory and start new projects and ventures. They have a burning desire to be the first to venture into a new field.

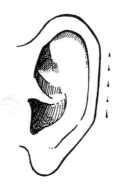

Figure 14   High Pioneering Trend

Trait Combinations

When the Pioneering Trend is combined with high Tolerance (Figure 32) and Construction (Figure 53) the result may be taking on too many new projects instead of staying focused. When this trait is less evident on individuals, they do not have such a strong urge to break into new territory. If we were able to take a peek back into history, we might well observe definite patterns in the facial structure that reflected the pioneering spirit of the time.

Directing Pioneering Trend

Remember to stay focused or you may find your efforts are diluted by too many projects.

ADVENTUROUS

This trait is found by how much the cheek bones protrude from the sides and the front of the face. Adventurous people love excitement and change. They want to be where things are happening and get physical excitement from new experiences. They enjoy variety in their day, and love to travel. In repetitive situations they are quickly bored.

Figure 15   High Adventurousness

Those with high Adventurous traits need a variety of tasks in their jobs, particularly if they are also High Tolerance (Figure 32). The Adventurous child needs constant change and excitement. If this is not found, they may get into mischief just for the thrill of it.

It's All in the Face

Involve them in sports or hobbies where they show a strong interest. Make sure the adventurous child's day has a variety of activities.

Examples of those with high Adventurousness are are Hilary Clinton, Sophia Loren, Margaret Thatcher, Newt Gingrich and Barbara Walters.

People who score low on Adventurousness are more content to stay at home. It may cause a problem in a marriage when one person scores high on adventurous and the other low. One will want to be on the move and the other will prefer to stay with what feels familiar. Adventurous people will feel that the less adventurous are missing out on the excitement. However the less Adventurous derive their enjoyment from the quality of the experience itself, rather than the excitement it brings.

How to Direct Low Adventurousness

Be more willing to venture out in your life. Spend time with an adventurous person in an activity you both enjoy.

How to Direct High Adventurousness

Sometimes people who are high in Adventurousness become very restless. They may confuse their nomadic spirit with the need to live in many different locations. If you score high on this trait, use your free time to travel, or take up a hobby that gives you the variety you need.

Possible careers are flight attendant (notice the next time you fly how many attendants have this trait), travel agent, commissioned sales, international marketing, advertising, theatre (with Forward Balance).

AUTOMATIC GIVING

This trait is determined by the size of the lower lip in comparison to the size of the face. The larger the lip, the greater the generosity.

Fig. 16   High Automatic Giving

People who score high on Automatic Giving may find it difficult to receive. They do not allow others the pleasure of giving to them. Their generosity may work against them. They have a tendancy to over extend themselves both in time and money. They take on more than they can handle. Other people may rely heavily on them for both their time and money. People with this trait combined with Impulsiveness (Figure 25) may give away their last penny.

People who score low on Automatic Giving give more consideration in the act of giving. They may appear stingy or tight to others, or they may be seen as using and abusing other people's generosity.

Directing High Automatic Giving

Allow others the pleasure of giving to you. Think before you give or offer your services without charge. Don't let people take advantage of you.

Directing Low Automatic Giving

Learn to give to others without any strings attached. Give more of yourself in personal relationships, and spend more time helping others who would greatly appreciate your assistance.

It's All in the Face

PRIDE IN PERSONAL APPEARANCE

This is shown by the shortness of the area above the lip to the base of the nose. The shorter it is, the stronger the need to look good and get attention based on appearance. Consequently these people enjoy clothes and may have an extensive wardrobe. They are also inclined to take things personally and do not accept criticism well. These people may appear to be extremely vain, and can't go by a mirror without checking their appearance.

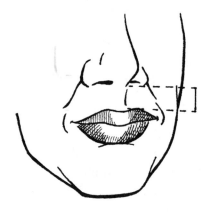

Figure 17   Pride in personal appearance

Trait Combinations
When Pride in Personal Appearace is combined with fine hair and design appretiation (the eyebrow has an inverted V) a person with these traits may enjoy a career as a clothing designer, interior design or image consultanting.

How to Direct Pride in Personal Appearance
Do not take it personally if your work comes under critisism. The person who is making the comments may be well intentioned, although their opinion was not solicited.

DRY WIT

This is shown by the length above the lip to the base of where the nose joins the lip. When the length above the lip is longer in comparison to the size of the face, this indicates a dry sense of humor. This trait reflects the opposite of Pride in Personal Appearance.

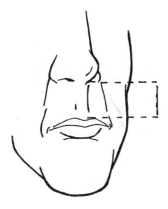

Figure 18   Dry Wit   A Dry sense of Humor

People who have this trait are more concerned with getting the job done, rather than how they look. They are less interested in the current clothing trends, and are the personal shoppers' dream clients because there is so much potential to reach. They get so wrapped up in what they're doing that dressing is the last thing on their minds.

How to Direct Dry Wit

Never use your dry wit at anyone in a way that could cause hurt feelings. When buying clothes, hire a personal shopper.

AUTOMATIC RESISTANCE

A more accurate term for this trait is stubbornness. People whose jaws look wedge shaped (pointed chin) automatically resist under any pressure. They appear to handle pressure much better than most. However because they keep things bottled up inside them while seemingly handling a situation, they often eventually experience medical problems from internalizing the stress they are under.

Fig. 19 High automatic resistance   *Fig. 20 Low automatic resistance*

When people with high Automatic Resistance are pushed into action, they will put up strong resistance. The more they are pushed the less favorable the results will be. When this trait is in a young child, explain to them the benefits gained by doing something rather than saying "You have to. That's why.". These children (as well as adults) need motivating reasons and explanations and they'll come around. Ross Perot and Prince Charles are some good examples of high Automatic Resistance.

When the jaw is less pointed, people tend to be more agreeable and compliant in the moment. They give in more easily to pressure or persuasion, although that does not mean they like what is happening. Low Automatic Resistance is indicated when the point of the chin is very square. People who have this trait tend to be more pugnacious, and enjoy a fight whether verbally or physically. Generally they are more compliant and do not work well under pressure.

Directing High Automatic Resistance

When dealing with people who have high Automatic Resistance, do not apply pressure. Discuss the situation at hand. Find out the reasons for their objections or beliefs. These people do not like being forced into situations. Use a more persuasive approach, rather than a forceful one.

If you are a person with High Automatic Resistance, consider a situation before automatically saying no. What are you gaining by being stubborn without justification? Ask yourself what it is that you are resisting? Is it based on principle or feelings?

Directing Low Automatic Resistance

People with low Automatic Resistance are generally easier to get along with and easier to influence. They are more open and co-operative. If you have low Automatic Resistance, make it known how you feel when the pressure is negative. If the pressure seems overwhelming, just take a moment and see what can be done immediately. Then make a plan for completing the project. The pressure may be due to procrastination. Make an effort and do what is needed to be done in the moment.

ADMINISTRATIVE versus MINISTRATIVE

The straight or hooked (convex) nose shows an Administrative nature, whereas when the ridge of the nose next to the eyes dips down (concave) this indicates a Ministrative nature.

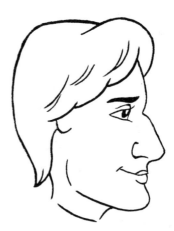

Figure 21   *Ministrative*
Concave

Figure 22   *Administrative*
Convex

Administrative people like to oversee a project rather than to ministrate (ie to serve). They do not enjoy a job where they are in service such as waiting, nursing, sales assistant, or at the beck and call of others. They prefer to hire and organize the services of others rather than do the job themselves, especially when that means being subservient to others. They make good delegators.

Adminisratives are concerned with the best price. They are bargain hunters, value is extremely important to them. This does not necessarily imply they will settle for an inferior product.

Possible careers would be financial investments, real estate, stock brokerage, business administration and raising money for charities.

Trait Combinations

When high Administrativeness is combined with Acquisitiveness (Figure 30) these people would hold on to their investments. They put money and business first. Examples of high Administration are Margaret Thatcher, Dustin Hoffman, Aristotle Onasis, Ross Perot. Ministrative people are more spontaneous and enjoy helping others. They are the people who like to volunteer.

Trait Combinations

Combine Ministrativeness with high tolerance (Figure 31) and their services may get abused because of their willingness to help. When this trait is combined with low acquisitiveness, they tend not to balance the check books. They may give away their last penny. Possible careers are nursing, ministry, YMCA, physician, secretary, volunteer work, and waiter/waitress.

Directing Administrativeness

If you are an Administrative person, do not put a price tag on everything. Consider offering your own time and learn to enjoy the reward of helping someone. If you also score low in Automatic Giving (Figure 16) donate to an organization which you know will invest the money well. When working with High Administrative people, know that they will be more concerned with the price, they'll look for a bargain.

Directing Ministrativeness

If you are more Ministrative, think first before offering your services without charge. People will place more value on services when they have to pay for them. Do not over extend yourself. Remember to save time for yourself and your family.

CONCISE/VERBOSE

This trait is identified by the fullness or thinness of the upper lip. The thinner the upper lip, compared to the lower one, the more Concise a person is, the fuller the upper lip the more Verbose.

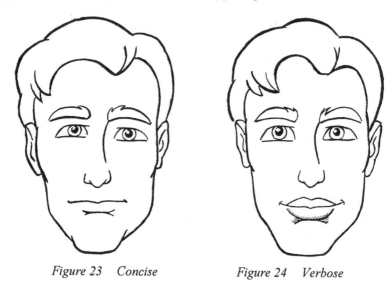

Figure 23   Concise   *Figure 24   Verbose*

This trait shows the brevity of expression. People who score high on this trait are more concise, and may even be perceived as terse in their verbal expression. They come to the point with fewer words and do not like repetitious conversation.   Politicians are good examples of Conciseness, as are heads of large companies such as Lee Iacoca.   They are very specific and direct, and do not like to waste words. This may be interpreted as being short or rude by others, or lacking diplomacy. The advantage of concise people is that they can give clear, precise and easy to follow directions. It is also observed as a developed rather than inherited trait in people who have had a very hard life either physically or emotionally, making them appear tough. When the mouth is both thin and small in comparison to the whole design of the face, this shows someone who is extremely introverted and may be considered shy.

People who have larger upper lips tend to be more verbose. They are built to express themselves more easily. They embroider conversation with adjectives, adverbs and emotion, and consequently may bore others with too much detail. This verbosity may cause a problem when dealing with people who are more concise, because when given more information than needed, the concise person loses interest in the conversation. The positive aspect of verbosity is that these people can speak at length easily when required. Their speech is more colourful and flowing. They need to avoid repetition or listeners may become bored. Examples of Verbosity are Jimmy Carter, Mick Jagger and Princess Ann.

Trait Combinations

People who are Verbose and Impetuous (lips protruding forward) make good story tellers.

Directing Conciseness

If you are a very concise person, when working or talking with others who are more verbose, embellish your conversation with more adjectives, fill them in with more details than you would normally use. Ask specific questions, suggest you want to get to the point directly. Try to be patient with verbose people, and listen closely to the content of the conversation. What you are doing is creating a bond by acknowledging others needs.

Directing Verbosity

If you are verbose, use fewer words and quickly get to the point when talking with a concise person. Organize your thoughts before speaking.

IMPULSIVENESS

The lips are the physical indicator for Impusiveness. As you look at a person's profile, notice the position of the lips in relation to the glabella (the ridge of the nose). When looking at the profile of the face, do the lips project forward or recede? Take a ruler and line up with the ridge of the nose, making sure the head is level. If the lips can be clearly viewed, the person is very impulsive, spontaneous and jump into situations without much thought.

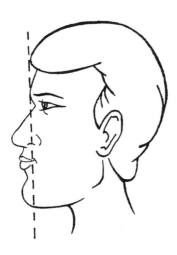

Figure 25   High Impulsive

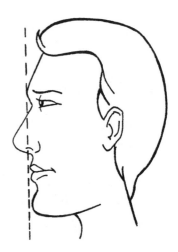

Figure 26   Low Impulsive

Those with a high Impulsive trait, tend to interrupt conversations, and may bring up something from out of the blue. They are inclined to impulse buying and need to ask themselves first whether they really need to purchase this item. They may need to learn to   step back and take time to consider first before accepting another invitation or taking on another project.

Trait Combinations

Combine this trait with Credulity (Figure 27) and a person with these traits may commit themselves to something they might regret later. An example is John McEnroe.

Combine Impulsiveness with Objectiveness (Figure 51) and now you have a very fast impulsive decision maker. Add the trait low Acquisitiveness, (this is a person whose ears lay flat against their head, as opposed to protruding, see Figure 50) and Risk-Taker to these traits, you now have a formula for a gambler, or someone who has a hard time saving money and is constantly getting into debt. Possible careers for the highly Impulsive are radio, TV, (combined with high Self-Confidence) teaching (with low Tolerance), interpreter, sales.

People whose lips recede behind the glabella tend to be more calculated in thought and action. They are more deliberate and not prone to quick or impetuous decisions. People with low Impulsiveness and Sequential Thinking (Figure 52) will take time to consider a major buying decision.

Directing Impulsiveness

If you are Impulsive, look before you leap or you may regret that decision. Learn not to interrupt a conversation. Pay attention to what is being said, and allow the other person to complete their comment or response. Count to ten before you say anything and leave more of your thoughts unspoken.

Directing Low Impulsiveness

If you are low Impulsive, you may want to consider being more spontaneous, loosening up and going with the spirit of the occasion.

CREDULITY/SKEPTICISM

The physical indicator is the nose viewed from the profile. When the tip of the nose turns upwards, this shows Credulity. This person is more gullible than one with a turned-down nose (indicating Skepticism).

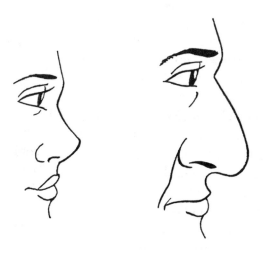

Figure 27   Credulity   Figure 28   Skepticism

Gullible people have an instinctive trust in what is told to them They may find themselves taken in by others taking advantage of this trait. They can be naive, and seldom check out credentials, background or authority. On the positive side they are more trusting, open minded, and willing to give new ideas a trial. When considering investments they need to consciously demand proof and get second opinions before committing themselves or their money.

Skeptical people are less open minded. They automatically doubt or question what is being said, and do not accept things at face value. To some people they may appear distrustful or even hostile. If you need to convince them, make sure you completely satisfy their questions and you can win them over. The positive aspect of skeptisism is that this person will thoroughly question the reason to buy.

Trait Combinations

Combine this trait with Analyticalness, and these people may be considered very opinionated. Well-known examples of the combination are Ross Perot, John Lennon, Bob Hope, Meryl Streep, and Steven Spielberg.

Directing Credulity

If you are Credulous, ask more questions when considering a purchase. Do not be taken in by a "good deal". Ask someone who has knowledge about the product or opportunity. A person with high Credulity and Impulsiveness, may find themselves making a purchase they regret later.

How to Direct Skeptics

When you are dealing with people who are skeptical, remember they have a psychological need for proof or substantiation. When presenting them with a new idea or concept, make sure you present them with all the important facts. They need facts so that they can make up their own minds.

If you are a skeptical person, try to be more open and listen to other people's ideas, and get the whole story and all the facts before judging or making up your mind.

FEELINGS AND EMOTIONS

- Self-Confidence
- Tolerance
- Self Reproach
- Exactingness
- Methodicalness
- Sharpness
- Forward/Backward Balance
- Detail Concern
- Mental/Physical Motive
- Sound and Music Appreciation
- Dramatic Appreciation
- Emotional Expression
- Discrimination
- Mood Swings
- Esthetic Appreciation
- Acquisitiveness

Confidence plays an important part
in our self esteem
and will flourish in a supportive environment

SELF-CONFIDENCE

The physical indicator is width of the face. This is determined by the vertical ledge or bone which is located at the outer edge of both eyebrows.   The width of the face from this outer edge is compared with the length of the face. High Self-Confidence is seen when the face is very wide at this location. The difference between this trait and Authoritativeness, is that the Self-Confident person likes a challenge, whereas the Authoritative person (Figure 9) likes to be in charge.

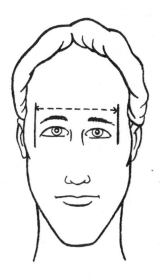
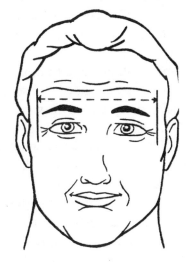

Figure 29   Low Self-Confidence   *Figure 30   High Self-Confidence*

It's All in the Face

People with high Self-Confidence enjoy a challenge, and focus on results rather than difficulties. If you were to walk into a meeting you could spot them right away - they look in charge. If people with this trait also have high Authoritativeness (Figure 9) this will add to their leadership qualities. Wearing a suit that is extremely formal adds to their power. Examples are Hilary Clinton, Barbara Bush, and Boris Yeltsin.

Women who possess high Self-Confidence may need to be careful wearing a strong red suit. Men are not always comfortable with the strength of this message and it may bias feelings before a meeting has begun. However if this is the woman's intention and she is confident of her position, then enjoy . . . Assess the situation and make a decision what to wear based on the task.

High Self-Confidence people are courageous and enjoy life on a large scale. They assume they can tackle anything and will do so with very little hesitation, or concern for confrontations. One of their biggest risks is running headlong into each other. They may appear intimidating to those people who have narrower features (lower Self-Confidence) because they lead life on a much grander scale. They are very assured people and can make good leaders.

Their lesson in life is to learn not to prejudge others with less Self-Confidence. They should not expect them to take on a task outside their expertise until they have all the facts and knowledge to carry out the project. If high Self-Confidence is not handled well, some people when put into a management position may become overpowering and intimidating, particularly if they wear strong colours that further amplify their presence. They may expect others to achieve more than is reasonable. They need to know that it is important to work as a team, work with their people rather than as a manager on a throne.

Examples of Trait Combinations

Consider people with high Self-Confidence and high Physical Insulation; these traits could work for or against them. On the reinforcing side, not only are they confident about what they are doing, they do not let situations affect their emotions. For example Clinton has high Self-Confidence traits and high Physical Insulation (Figure 5) whereas Bush has lower Self-Confidence and finer hair. If you were to see the two together, without knowing who they were, you would notice that Clinton would appear to be the more confident person of the two. When high Self-Confidence is combined with high Authoritativeness, these are the people who take charge. Examples are Hilary Clinton and Barbara Bush.

Low Self-Confidence

People with narrower faces can develop a learned Self-Confidence through knowledge and experience. By nature, however, they are the support people in a group, and may not necessarily be comfortable in a leadership situation. They are much more aware of what is going on around them and how different situations can affect them and other people. They are more aware of their limitations, and stay with what is familiar until they have enough knowledge to take major steps forward. These people have narrow faces and do not carry as much perceived authority as those with wider faces. However if they have extremely sharp features and are very forceful, they appear to be more self-confident.

Take, for example, people with low Self-Confidence and low Physical Insulation. If their work was highly criticized, not only would they internally feel like failures, they would lose what little confidence they had. This is often a situation that occurs in childhood development, when the child does not live up to the expectations of a parent and is constantly criticized. The lesson for those with Low Self-Confidence is not to take criticism too personally and express to the other person their feelings about the situation. Low self-confident people often undersell themselves. They take off-handed comments personally and may over react to small issues. In public appearance they feel ill at ease in the

It's All in the Face

limelight, and are very sensitive to criticism of their presentations, often doubting their own capabilities.

Directing High Self-Confidence

If you are highly Self-Confident, learn to respect other people's knowledge. Be aware of others, and listen to what they are saying. When in a group situation allow others to voice their opinion. Although another person may seem meek and mild, they may have something important to contribute. Do not discount them.

Directing Low Self-Confidence

When asked to take on a new project, find out every thing you need to know. Consult with others who have experience in the related area. Take one step at a time. Let people know what you have accomplished and enjoy the attention. If feelings of low Self-Confidence become a barrier to getting things done, then set out to achieve goals that are obtainable. If the goals cannot be changed, then set a series of milestones so that the final goal is reached as a series of smaller accomplishments. Since knowledge and understanding promote confidence, find out all you need to know before launching a project or getting into a new situation. When you find yourself with uncertain feelings, ask whether this is rational, stop and look to see what can be done to change those thought patterns.

TOLERANCE

This trait is represented by the distance between the eyes, and determines how much a person will tolerate a situation. When making this measurement, you also need to consider the size of the eye. Can a whole eye fit into the space between the two eyes? If so, and there is space left over, then this is a very Tolerant person. If it just fits, then this is a person who is just tolerant. If the space between the eyes is less than an eye width, then this person has very low Tolerance.

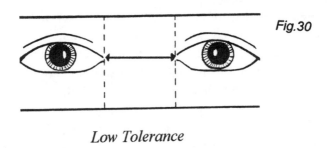

Fig.30

Low Tolerance

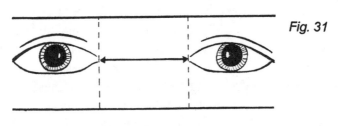

Fig. 31

High Tolerance

It's All in the Face

The people with high Tolerance are more permissive, both of themselves and of others. There is a tendency to put things off until tomorrow. Avoiding procrastination is their biggest challenge. They put up with situations too long, and need to let others know sooner how they feel, otherwise, people take advantage of their good nature. They tend to be more relaxed and not to overreact to less tolerant situations.They are more interested in the big picture (macro vision). These people may get easily distracted by what is going on around them and find it hard to stay focused.

When high Tolerance is combined with low Concentration in school children, they may have a short attention span. Until the child and its parents have an understanding that this is a part of their genetic make up, these traits in action may be interpreted as disruptive. When all parties understand what is going on, the situation can be handled in a much more constructive way. The first step would be to have the child's personology chart made, then discuss the results in a group session with the teacher, parents and child.

The high Tolerance individuals are procrastinators, and may find themselves running late for appointments because they want to do just one more thing. Their friends and associates may consider them unreliable, when they are really trying to fit in too many activities. Consequently, they over-extend themselves and end up cancelling at the last moment, or turning up late for the appointment. Combine this trait with Impetuousness and this could get them into serious trouble. They need to respect other people's time, and if they're going to be late then call ahead. Think first before accepting all those invitations or volunteering for different causes. Examples of high Tolerance are Hilary Clinton, Brooke Shields, Jimmy Carter and Boris Yeltsin. Although models are probably not picked for their tolerance level, this trait is a dominant characteristic in these people. Next time you look at a magazine, notice how most of them have widely spaced eyes.

Low Tolerance people are much more focused on the issues at hand; they are interested in the micro picture. They have an intense "now" reaction and have a built-in sense of right and wrong. If they are presented with too many tasks at once they may get frustrated, they are better at handling one job at a time. They get irritated very quickly and do not appreciate being interrupted from what they are doing. They are much more focused on what is happening now. If you want a job done well, then assign it to low Tolerance people. They will stay focused until the job is completed, unwilling to tolerate interruptions, distractions and poor quality. These people make excellent teachers and supervisors, because they do not let situations get out of control. They like a job done well and on schedule. An example of low Tolerance is Barbara Streisland.

Combination Traits

People with fine hair (sensitive, low Physical Insulation) and low Tolerance will have their tolerance reduced still further. If someone arrives late for an appointment they will be extremely annoyed and consider the visitor to be inconsiderate of their time, whatever the reason.

Directing High Tolerance

If you are a high Tolerance person and find yourself working with a low Tolerance people, try not to introduce too many ideas at once - just stay focused on one or two things. When you give the low tolerance person a job to do, you can count on them to stay focused (even though you might not) on what they are doing until it is finished.

Set boundaries and deadlines, and stick to them. Do not put things off to tomorrow. Try not to over commit yourself. Make sure you arrive on time for appointments. If you find yourself running late, call ahead of time to let people know.

It's All in the Face

Directing Low Tolerance

If you are a low Tolerance person, you may over react without realizing it. Things annoy you, so relax and take a deep breath. Refocus your thoughts or move away from the situation, get some exercise or change the thought pattern. Respond instead of reacting. Do not let minor irritations upset you. Learn to put situations in perspective. Because you see something as not being right, this may not be how others see it.

When working with high Tolerance people, make it known that they need to complete the project on time. Let them know why the project is important, and the consequences of delaying its completion.

SELF REPROACH

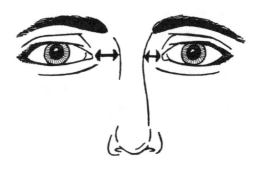

Figure 33   Self-Reproach

76

Self-Reproach is experienced only when there is a swing mood on tolerance. This trait is shown when one eye is closer to the bridge of the nose than the other. People with this trait tend to be unpredictable. They feel an inconsistency in their tolerance level. One never knows what to expect. One moment situations do not seem to bother them, then another time they are irritated by every little thing. This may be puzzling to those around them, as they are not sure what to expect. The people themselves never know how they will react. When they react irrationally, whether at work or at home, they are hard on themselves for behaving in such a manner.

Directing Self-Reproach

Understanding your swing in tolerance levels will help you to get better control of your reactions. You can control the mood. Remember to try to respond rather than react.

EXACTINGNESS

The physical indicator is the vertical furrow between the eyebrows and represents the desire for precision. The longer the furrow the higher the score. This physical trait is developed (rather than inherited) by repeated muscular tension from prolonged concentration.

People who score high on Exactingness are concerned with the information being exact, precise and accurate. They like to check and recheck everything they do until they are convinced everything is correct. They may be considered too fussy by others when a situation does not need such scrutiny.

Possible vocations that demand exactingness and tend to develop this trait are proof-reading, auditing, computer programming, accounting, investigating, diamond cutting, and dental work.

Figure 34   *Exactingness*

Trait Combinations

When this trait is combined with high Tolerance (Figure 30) a person has to put a greater emphasis on focusing and getting things exactly right. This is often seen in actors and actresses, which may be due to the demands made of them during their work.

Directing Exactingness

If you are an exacting person, try to relax when working on projects. Recognize when you are fussing over unimportant or irrelavent details.

Directing Low Exactingness

People who score low on this trait need to take particular care to re-check everything before giving the project their final approval.

METHODICALNESS

The physical expression of Methodicalness is observed directly above the eyebrows where a muscle has developed a ridge across the forehead. The trait is developed through intense concentration on a methodical process. Methodicalness can become an obsession starting as out Exactingness (Figure 34) and then progressing to Detail concern (Figure 39).

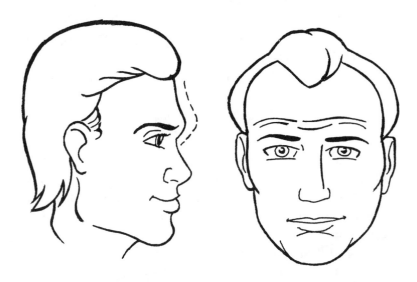

Fig. 35   Methodicalness High. Overly concerned with details

People with this trait like to complete each step before moving on. This is their routine way of doing things. They are not adaptable and become stuck in a rut because of the pattern they fall into. They like to have everything worked out beforehand, something which irritates people who need to have a project completed in a shorter time. Careers and hobbies which demand a meticulous step by step process develop this trait.
Trait Combinations

It's All in the Face

People with Methodicalness and Subjective Thinking (Figure 52) have an even slower thinking process. These people cannot be hurried, either in filling out forms or starting new projects.

Directing Methodicalness

If you are a methodical person, make a conscious effort to be more adaptable. Do not impose your routine on others. Deliberately re-arrange your routine from time to time, to get in touch with the more creative side.

Directing Low Methodicalness

Recognize the benefits of doing tasks in a step by step process. It may seem boring to you, however the outcome may be well worth the effort when a methodical process is used.

SHARPNESS

This trait is decided by the sharpness (angularity) of the facial features as seen from the profile. People who are sharp are very aware of what is going on around them. They have a sense of what is happening without being told, and enjoy ferreting out information.

Trait Combinations

When this trait is combined with Objectiveness (Figure51), Forward Balance (Figure 37), Impatience, and Low Tolerance (Figure 31) this is likely to produce quick responses. A good example of this trait combination in action is the Prosecuting attorney for the O.J.Simpson case, Marcia Clark. She is well known for her success in wining criminal cases. Other examples are Meryl Streep and Prince Philip.

Careers for this combination could be accounting, law, investigation, quality control, inspection, FBI agent.

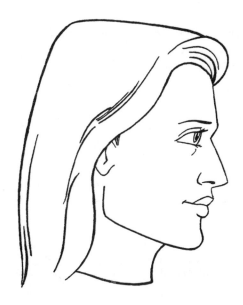

Figure 36   *Sharpness*

FORWARD/BACKWARD BALANCE

This trait is shown by how much face there is appearing in front of the ear in comparison to the amount behind the ear to the back of the head. This is best seen from the side view. When there is more face in front, this is known as Forward Balance.

People with Forward Balance think in terms of the present and the future. There is a strong need for recognition and appreciation. They enjoy being on stage whether it is giving a presentation, teaching or in the theatre. They need praise and acknowledgement. To others they may be perceived as "stealing the show". They need to allow others the opportunity for recognition and contribution. These people are less considerate of others. This trait is seen in many juvenile offenders. They enjoy the spotlight and recognition that comes from their peer group. Once their traits

81

have been positively directed, they may well become upstanding members in the community.

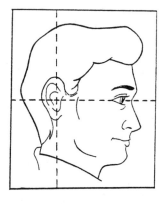
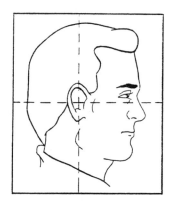

Figure 37   Forward Balance   *Figure 38   Backward Balance*

Backward Balance is shown by how far forward the ear is set on the face. People with Backward Balance relate to what has historically happened and live in the present. They rely on past experiences and accomplishments. It is harder for them to plan long term projects. Although people who score high on Backward Balance are more considerate, they have a tendancy to hold grudges over a long period of time. They enjoy working in the background and have a harder time selling themselves.

They are less concerned with what others think and more interested in what they are doing. They are not very concerned themselves about recognition. At the same time they may resent being overlooked.

Careers for Forward Balance could be radio commentator, model, master of ceremonies, actor/actress, racing, teaching. Careers for Backward Balance could be historian, cateering, librarian, history teacher.

Directing Forward Balance

If you have Forward Balance, remember to include others in the spotlight. Remember that not everyone wants to move at the same pace as yourself. Take classes in the theatre. Teach workshops. When working with others who are Backward Balance, direct the conversation so that the results you want will be acheived. For example, if the person you are working with fails to see the need for long term planning, explain to them the benefits gained by maping out the furture for business or family activities.

Directing Backward Balance

If you have Backward Balance, learn to let go of what has happened, it's "water under the bridge". Do not bore others with your repeated conversation of what others have done to you. Forgive and forget. Blow your own trumpet, let people know what you are doing and accomplishing. Take advantage of new opportunities.

DETAIL CONCERN

This trait is indicated by the noticeable development of small mounds above each side of the inner eyebrow. It indicates that a person is constantly paying attention to detail. This trait is developed through work or creative activity, rather than inherited. It is common in computer programmers, dentists, accountants, diamond cutters, surgeons and anyone working with fine detail and precision. People who score high on this trait may become obsessed by detail. Their co-workers and family might find this frustrating, because at times it interferes with a job being completed.

It's All in the Face

Suitable careers for people who have Detail Concern would be accounting, editing, drafting and computer design.

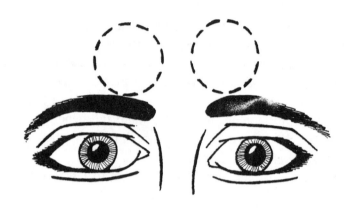

Figure 39   *Detail Concern*

Directing High Detail Concern
If you are over concerned with detail, keep it in perspective and ignore it when it is not important. Do not impose your concern for detail on family or relationships.
Directing Low Detail Concern
When Detail Concern is important to another person, make the extra effort and pay attention to details even though they are unimportant to you.

MOTIVE (PHYSICAL/MENTAL MOTIVE)

The indicator for Physical and Mental Motive is the length from the base of the chin to the base of the nose in comparison to the length of the face. When it is long a person reponds physically to situations, rather than mentally, and has Physical Motive.

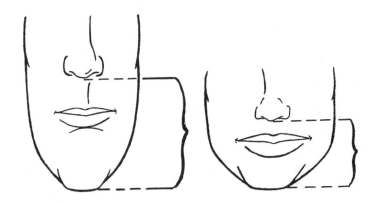

Figure 40   Physical Motive   *Figure 41   Mental Motive*

People who score high on Physical Motive like to be where the action is, and to be physically active. It is harder for them to slow down and relax. They have so much energy that sometimes they do not know what to do with themselves. Without high physical activity they quickly become bored and restless, and it is hard for them to sit still for long. When Physical Motive is combined with high Foot Dexterity (Figure 1) this amplifies the need for high physical activity. People who have a lower need for physical outlet may find it harder to keep up with them. Many sports players are extremely physical people, for example Joe Montana, Jimmy

It's All in the Face

Connors, Boris Becker, Chris Everett, Virginia Wade and Gerard Dépardieu.

People who score high on Mental Motive (the space is shorter from the base of the chin to the base of the nose) are stimulated by mental challenges. Mental activity is as consuming to them as physical activity is to the physically motivated. They accomplish more through the mental process than through physical action. Without a mental challenge they may become bored in their jobs. It takes them longer to recover from high physical activity. Their physical side may be neglected because of their strong desire for mental activity. Just as the physical person needs to take time out to use their mind, so the people who are more mentally motivated need to take time to exercise.

Directing Physical Motive

People who are more Physically Motivated need to strike a balance of rest and exercise. Others who score low on this trait will find it difficult to keep up the same pace.

Directing Mental Motive

Balance your mental activity with physical needs. Make sure you set time aside for physical exercise. When you are involved with high physical activity for long periods, make sure you take time out to rest.

SOUND AND MUSIC APPRECIATION

This trait is decided by the outer helix of the ear. When the outer edge is curved without any notch, the appreciation of music is high. If the inner rim is also completely round without the slightest notch, this indicates pitch and the ability to play an instrument.

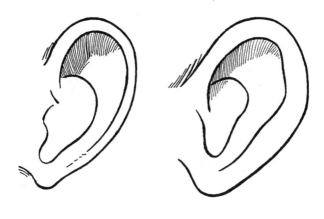

Figure 42   Music Appreciation   *Figure 43   Low Pitch Ability*

When Musical Appreciation is combined with fine hair and Esthetic Appreciation (Figure 49) this person will have a heightened sensitivity and appreciation of music. When you next see a musical group, notice the roundness of the outer and inner

It's All in the Face

edges of the ear. You will find that many musicians will have this trait along with high Esthetic Appreciation. An example is Luciano Pavarotti.

Children who have low pitch ability struggle for years to master an instrument with limited success. Yet their parents insist they continue with the music lessons, not realizing that this is not a natural activity for their child. People who have a high music appreciation love to attend concerts and listen to music for the greater part of the day. The first thing they do when getting into a car is to turn on the radio. People with Music Appreciation and fine hair tend to keep the music low key. However, when this trait is combined with coarse hair, they are more likely to turn up the volume.

Directing Low Music Appreciation

Do not insist that the child has to take music lessons. Let them make the decision. Consider another activity the child will really enjoy. We are not all born to become Mozart or Pavarotti.

Directing High Music Appreciation

Encourage children who have this innate ability to take lessons, and if they are teenagers to form a musical group.

DRAMATIC APPRECIATION

Dramatic Appreciation is indicated by how much the eyebrow rises above the orbital bone (top of the eye socket). Examples are Doctor Spock and Boris Yeltsin When you look at them face on you will notice the eyebrows go upwards.

Figure 44   Dramatic Appreciation

People with Dramatic Appreciation exaggerate both verbally and physically when expressing themselves. They over dramatize their feelings and emotions and at times appear theatrical and even insincere. People who have this trait with Verboseness (Figure 24) make good story tellers.

Their dramatic flare shows in their style of dress and the interior design of their homes and offices. People who have high Dramatic Appreciation are at home in the theatre, teaching seminars or in any situation where they have a captive audience.

Directing Dramatic Appreciation

The dramatic person's challenge is to know when to keep things simple, and to stay with the facts without dramatic embellishment. Use this talent for presentations or the theatre. Keep the drama in check, and use when needed to emphasize a point or situation.

EMOTIONAL EXPRESSION

Emotional Expression is found by the size of the iris in relationship to the sclera (white of the eye). The larger the iris, the greater is the amount of emotion that is outwardly expressed. People with a high score are more likely to show and express what they feel to a greater degree. They are more affectionate and display more warmth and feelings whether showing sorrow, happiness or enthusiasm. At times they are extreme in their emotional expression.

Figure 45

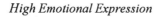

High Emotional Expression   *Low Emotional Expression*

Trait Combinations

When Emotional Expression is combined with fine hair, the feelings are amplified. People with this trait combination may feel intensely other people's sadness, although they may not know the people involved in the tragedy. They are greatly moved by what is happening around them. Because their emotions are more obvious, it doesn't necessarily mean that their inner feelings are any stronger than those of a person who is less emotionally expressive. They find themselves "wrapped up" in their emotions, and the situation may get out of perspective.

People who score low on Emotional Expression are able to deal more dispassionately with others. They make decisions with the head rather than with the heart. Their eyes are less expressive, and may appear indifferent, cold or unemotional. They feel as deeply as an emotionally expressive person, but they keep their feelings under the surface. Low Emotional Expressive people are not as outwardly affectionate and find it difficult to express what they feel. They stay outwardly calm and work well in situations where emotions are getting out of control.

Directing Low Emotional Expression

People with low expressiveness will benefit by showing their affections more openly, and letting others know how they feel. When the feelings are not revealed by facial expression, it is perfectly acceptable to use words instead.

Directing High Emotional Expression

Women who have high emotional expression may be perceived by men as flirtatious and inviting sexual advancement. This can be avoided with body language, physical distancing and toning down the emotional level of communication.

In a sales situation where the customers are more emotionally expressive, interact with them on an emotional level. Notice the amount of expression in their eyes, this will tell you how the sale or presentation is progressing.

DISCRIMINATION

Discrimination is the compulsion to be more selective. It is measured by the distance from the top rim of the eyelid to the base of the brow. The greater the distance between the two, the more discriminating or selective the person. Discriminating people appear more formal, reserved and less approachable. Others who are more affable, may consider these people to be snobbish and less accessible.

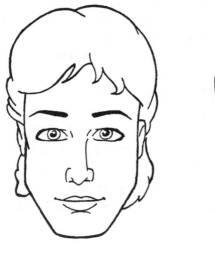 

Figure 47   Discrimination   *Figure 48   Affableness*

A person who is more discriminating will take time to consider all aspects of a situation before making a commitment, whether it is the friends they have around them, the purchases they make, or other life situations. Do not try to rush these people into a decision, they need more time to consider if this is something they really want to do. Examples are Warren Christopher, Jackie Onasis, Boris Yeltsin.

Less discriminating people are more affable, and less selective in the people they have around them, and the products they purchase. They establish an immediate rapport and make friends easily. They will touch people on the arm or give them a spontaneous hug. An example is the tennis player André Agassi.

Trait Combinations

Combine low Discrimination with Impetuousness and this will amplify the effect. People who have this trait combination may jump into partnership which they regret later. Think first before approaching people, otherwise a situation may end up getting out of control.

Directing Affableness

When less discriminating (affable) people interact with those who are more discriminating, they need to remember not to become too familiar and casual. Let the discriminating person make the first step, and do not be over friendly or they will initially retreat. Ask "permission" before entering their space. When in their home do not invade their space (see ten-acre principle). Be more formal on first contact with high Discrimination people. Do not make physical contact unless you really know them. Be more selective when choosing friends or making a purchase.

Directing Discrimination

If you are Discriminating, quickly put others at ease. Practice being more friendly. Colours you wear create formal or informal messages. When you want to appear more approachable, wear softer colours.

MOOD SWINGS

The more significant the differences between the two sides of the face, the greater the Mood Swings. People with mood swings are unpredictable. One moment they are on cloud nine and the next down in the dumps or plunging down to a depressive state.

Figure 48   *Mood Swings*

Too much caffeine or other drugs may create the mood shift. However, this may happen without any outside influences causing this swing. They may feel quite different about what they are doing, from one moment to the next. Learning how to manage this tendancy is the key to a more balanced life. Mood Swings reflect the differences in the parents. When one parent is so different physically from the other, the sibling may inherit opposite traits from each. On the positive side, people who score high on mood swings have a broader range of interests and are very versatile.

Because of these mood swings they are less consistent. At times the differences are so great, they may even doubt their own sanity. Within a family this may cause emotional problems. Once the person with high Mood Swings has a personology chart made, they have a better grasp of what is happening. Rather than seeing this as an uncontrolable problem, they now have a better understanding of the cause. Consequently, they can gain better control over their lives.

Exercising, changing the inner conversation, reading a book or just moving away from the situation or environment will help a person cope with these unexpected mood changes.

Directing Mood Swings

When you feel a change, take a break, change the activity, even if it is just for a few minutes. Don't make any important decision during this time. You are the only one who can actively do anything about it. Be alert to situations that trigger moods swings. It may even be diet. Establish goals that will keep you on track. This is important, particularly if you are starting a business. This is a time when you experience yourself going through the many peaks and valleys typical of a new businesses. Know that you can stabilize these mood swings. Do your creative work when in a high mood.

ESTHETIC APPRECIATION

High Esthetic Appreciation is shown when the eyebrows form a straight line that extends beyond the outer corner of the eye. This shows the need for environmental and emotional balance and harmony.

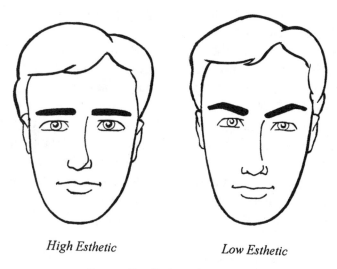

High Esthetic   *Low Esthetic*

Figure 49   Esthetic Appreciation

Balance and harmony are extremely important for people with high Esthetic Appreciation. When there is a lack of harmony in the lives of esthetics they may seek drugs or alcohol to create a so-called harmony (or to dull the discord). Teenagers and adults who are highly esthetic, fall victim to substance abuse when their home environment is out of balance; it is a way of escape. They drink for the feeling it gives them, despite the outcome. They seek to lose themselves, rather than identify and deal with what is real. Until they are willing to take responsibility, they are prisoners to their own senses. They need to look at the reason their lives are out of balance otherwise the situation can get out of hand.

High Esthetics are often passionately interested in art, music and photography. They have a fine sense of balance and harmony and quickly notice when things around them are not right.

People who have low Esthetic Appreciation are not so affected by their surroundings, they are able to cope better.

Directing Esthetic Appreciation

Be responsible for yourself and learn to take charge. Do not get caught up in a situation where the activity is controlling your life. Get in touch with yourself through Yoga, Tai Chi, meditation classes or walking. Take up a hobby that is an extension of your personal expression.

This trait is seen in many models, musicians and artists. Examples are Elvis Presley, Brooke Shields, Dustin Hoffman, Newt Gingrich and John Major.

ACQUISITIVENESS

Acquisitiveness is determined by how much of the ear lobe can be seen when looking at a person face on. The more it is exposed, the higher is the score. As the lobe starts to lay flat against the head, the lower the score. People who score high on Acquisitiveness and Conservation (Figure 54) are the "pack rats". They love to collect things and are very possessive of what they acquire and seldom dispose of things. They enjoy playing the stock market.

High Acquisitiveness
Figure 50

Low Acquisitivness

They appear very selfish, and have a hard time parting with their possessions or money. They put their possessions first before family or friends. This trait is amplified when they also score high on Administrativness (Figure 22) and Conservation (Figure 54). At a young age they should be encouraged to start a savings account. Examples of Acquisitiveness are Prince Charles and his sons, and also Ross Perot.

Less acquisitive people are inclined to discard possessions, and avoid saving for the future. They enjoy throwing things out, and have a detachment from their possessions when they are no longer useful. If they are out shopping and have ten dollars left in their pockets, they will more than likely spend it on something although the item is not needed. Money flows through their fingers, and they often waste it on impulse buying. These people need to take classes on investments or financial planning or get professional assistance on the best ways to protect their money. If one side of the face is high on Acquisitiveness and the other side low, then there will be swing moods of alternate saving and splurging.

Hobbies are collections of any kind, such as stamps, rocks, dolls, coins and games that involve purchasing or acquiring property.

Careers that interest highly Acquisitive people are import/export, stock broker, real estate and banking.

Trait Combinations

High Acquisitiveness and Administrativeness people are good with investments. They will always look for a good bargain. People with a combination of low Acquisitiveness, Automatic Giving (Figure 16), Impetuousness (Figure 25), and Considerateness, will give away their last penny before thinking of themselves.

Directing High Acquisitiveness

If you are an acquisitive person, learn to share with others. Study investments. Remember you can enjoy your life today and still plan for tomorrow. When this trait is seen in children, encourage them to have a savings account. Talk to them about the importance of investments, and how the stock market works.

Directing Low Acquisitiveness

Take a class on investments. Discipline yourself to put aside some money each month. Buy only what you need. Do not give away or throw out other people's possessions. They may place a very high value on them, whether sentiment or price.

THINKING TRAITS

- **OBJECTIVE/SUBJECTIVE**
- **CONSTRUCTION/CONSERVATION**
- **IDEALIZING TREND**
- **ANALYTICAL**
- **CRITICAL PERCEPTION**
- **JUDGEMENT VARIATION**
- **RHETORIC**

It's All in the Face

When dealing with other people, it helps
to know not only what they think
but *how* they think.

OBJECTIVE/SUBJECTIVE

This trait is located at the front of the forehead, and is best viewed from the side profile. When the forehead is more vertical (upright), a person is more Subjective (or sequential), whereas a forehead that slopes back at an angle is more Objective. This does not describe intelligence, but the speed at which a person responds and processes information or reacts.

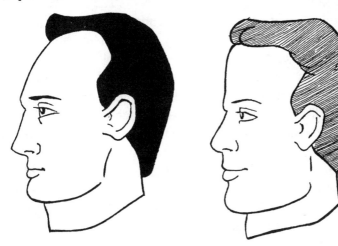

Figure 51   Objective Thinking   Figure 52   Subjective Thinking

The people who have a forehead that slopes back at an angle are more Objective, they jump quickly to conclusions, second guessing what other people are going to say or do. They respond quickly to what is happening around them and react well to emergencies. This trait is an asset in sports where quick reactions are needed, such as tennis or volley ball.

Objective people lack sequentialism, they do not evelute enough. They sometimes introduce related but unconsequential throught trends. When people score high on Objectiveness, they want quick results and appear impatient when others around them move at a slower pace. In contrast Subjective people often seem slow because they are more theoretical and reflective in their thinking. As children they have been known to play with mythical characters. When working with children who are Subjective, understand that they may need repetition in order to understand their work. Once this study pattern is established, they can do well in school.

Subjective thinkers go through a sequential process and use acquired knowledge more constructively. They need time to assimilate information. There is a tendency to blank out when learning under pressure. This may be a problem when taking exams. They need to prepare for tests several days beforehand, whereas Objective students like to cram at the last moment. People who are more sequential need to think through situations and do not like to be rushed. When a teacher goes too fast, the Sequential people are left behind. They are overwhelmed by the rapid delivery and shut down. Their inner conversation is that they're not as smart as the others because they can't keep up and get left behind. They need to give themselves plenty of time to review their work. Once the Subjective Thinking trait has been identified, both the student and the teacher can work more effectively together.

Sequential people are slower in their reactions to practical daily life situations. When they feel pressured, and others request them to speed up, it becomes overwhelming. When this trait is combined with an action trait such as high Physicalness, it will shorten the response time.

An example of a Subjective person is Ronald Reagan. Examples of Objective people are General Colin Powell and Margaret Thatcher.

Trait Combinations

Combine Subjective Thinking with low Self-Confidence, these people will take longer to launch a new concept or product.

However, once they have accumulated and understood the information, there is no hesitation, particularly when these traits are combined with high action traits such as Physicalness.

Possible careers for Objective people are airline pilot, emergency service,tennis, basketball, control tower operator, communications, car and motorcycle racing.

Directing Objective Thinking

If you are an Objective person, do not jump to conclusions. The temptation is to move ahead. Take time to listen and read through the material rather than skimming the surface. The Objective people handle emergencies well. However in the slower pace of daily life and work, they will benefit by taking more time to think things through, rather than jumping to conclusions.

Directing Subjective Thinking

If you are a Subjective thinker, prepare well before getting into new situations. When you feel pressured into an immediate decision, create a step by step plan systematically. This exercise will help alleviate the pressure. In a sales situation, do not try to pressure these people or they will leave without buying. Subjective people need to speed up the pace when working with those who are more Objective.

CONSTRUCTION and CONSERVATION

Construction describes how a person thinks, either outward towards challenge and new projects or inward towards maintenance and preservation.

Figure 53   Construction   *Figure 54   Conservation*

The physical indicator is the squareness or roundness on the outside edge of the forehead above the temples as seen from the front. An example of the Construction forehead is Ross Perot as distinct from the more rounded Conservation forehead of Jimmy Carter.

The person with a square forehead enjoys starting new projects, and in extreme cases do not complete or maintain them because of eagerness to start yet another project. The people who score high on construction like to work with new concepts. Their work becomes their hobby. Repetitious assignments quickly bore them. Once a project is completed, they want to move on to something new and challenging. They do not like to patch or repair, and prefer to tear down and start afresh. They like new ideas (replacing old ones), research, pioneering, new tools and materials.

Construction people are more interested in a career rather than working in the home. This sometimes causes a conflict with marital relationships. The husband prefers his wife to stay at home (or vice versa) and look after the children whereas the wife feels frustrated because her strong desire to have a job is not being fulfilled. People with a high Construction trait need to take an outside job or work out of the home to live a balanced life. They need a purpose to their day. Work becomes a hobby for them and others may perceive them as workaholics. They need to be reminded to play once in a while.

Careers: Research, construction, architecture and design.

Trait Combinations

When a person scores high on Construction and Physicalness (Figure 7) this indicates a strong driving force to initiate new projects. If High Tolerance is added to the previous traits, the individual may take on too many projects. Both the energy and focus will be less effective.

People with High Conservation and Growing Trend, are interested in environmental issues. They enjoy participating and leading workshops on personal growth. When those two traits are also combined with Sharp features (Figure 36) they are likely to be interested in nutrition and natural health foods. People with a high Conservation trait like to preserve what they have, and enjoy the creature comforts of home. The family and home are extremely important to them. They are the maintainers and nurturers and enjoy fixing up old things such as homes, furniture refinishing and renovating old cars. They are the pack rats,

It's All in the Face

inclined to hang on to everything in case it could be of use some day. People with high Conservation do not like wastage or spoilage, whereas the Construction person likes to start afresh rather than use what is at hand. Examples of Conservation are Bill Clinton, Princess Margaret.

Directing Construction

If you score high on construction, learn to make do with what is available. Don't be so hasty in discarding materials that could be used another day. Remember to put your family first sometimes. Surprise them.

Directing Conservation

If you are a person who scores high on Conservation, be more open to starting new projects or considering new ideas. Periodically go through your possessions, donate or throw out items you really have no use for.

Vocations: interior design, nursing, dentistry (with high hand co-ordination) catering, hotel operations, preservation and conservation of the environment, medicine, chemistry, social services and politics.

IDEALIZING TREND

The Idealizing Trend is shown by how low the ear is set on the face, and is measured by the distance from the aperture of the ear to the top of the head. The greater the distance, the stronger is the Idealizing Trend. Notice in Figure 55 how low the ear is set on the face compared with Figure 56. Idealists' heads are sometimes in the clouds. They are the dreamers, and may feel deeply about their aspirations.

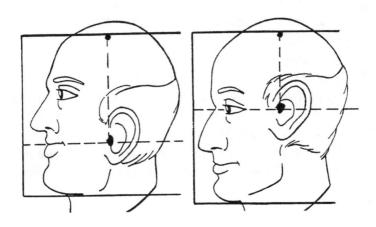

Figure 55   Idealistic   *Figure 56   Realistic*

They set high goals and ideals not only for themselves but for others. When their expectations fall short of what they expect, they feel let down. Highly idealistic people are so intensely involved with what they are doing, that they can lose sight of what is real. They do not always see the weaknesses in their ideal world. An example is John Tesh.

People who score low on Idealizing Trend are more practical and down to earth.   They set realistic standards for themselves and others, and are more interested in what needs to be done right now. Unlike idealistic people, they accept situations and people as they are, and are sometimes perceived as too relaxed and not interested in doing a thorough job.

Directing a High Idealizing Trend

If you have a high Idealizing Trend, learn to accept people and situations as they are. Do not impose your high standards on others. Not everyone has the same aspirations as yourself.

Directing a Low Idealizing Trend

If you have a low Idealizing Trend, never just make do, set higher standards for yourself. This will avoid disappointment.

ANALYTICAL

The analytical trait is determined by how much or how little of the eyelid is exposed. The more the eyelid is covered by the fold of the skin, the higher is the Analytical score. This person needs to know the reasons behind a situation. When the eyelid is more exposed, this person is less Analytical and more action driven.

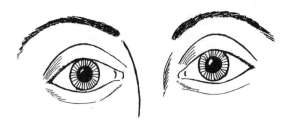

Figure 58   Low Analytical

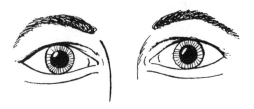

Figure 57   High Analytical

Analytical people need to look into all the different aspects of a situation or new purchase. They like to ferret out information, and will not act before they have gathered all the information needed to make a decision. They love to take things apart and figure out how they work. Combining the Analytical trait with Skepticism (Figure 28) increases the need for further information before accepting a new concept or product. When making a new purchase, they will research and compare quality, performance and price before the final decision is made. They enjoy analytical games, researching and analyzing information. Analytical people with sharp features may be viewed by others as extremely picky, e.g., Meryl Streep. Such people would make good investigators or FBI agents. Other examples of high Analytical are Paul Newman, Richard Gere and Princess Diana. People who are less Analytical prefer to act right away without asking too many questions. Long drawn-out explanations are boring to them. They are more matter of fact and to the point. Low Analytical people are sometimes considered ruthless because they like to get to the core of things quickly, ignoring the subtleties and different facets which others have meticulously researched for them.

Trait Combinations

When low Analytical is combined with low Emotionality and Inconsiderateness, this affect can be amplified to point of unkindness.

Directing High Analyticalness

If you are highly Analytical, spend less time analyzing when it is not necessary. Speed up the process. Understand when others do not feel this need to know everthing and get to the point quicker.

Directing Low Analyticalness

If you are not an Analytical person, then understand others' need to know all the pertinent information. Slow down the reaction time. Be prepared to explain in detail to people who are more analytical. Honor their need to know; and this will create a feeling of trust when in a selling situation. When you ask highly analytical people to take on a task, they may bombard you with questions. They have a compulsion to know more about your request.

CRITICAL PERCEPTION

Critical Perception is represented by the lower outer edge of the eye. If the outer edge is lower than the inner corner, this is an indicator of someone who is very critical, for example O. J. Simpson. Notice how the outer part of the eye is lower. When both the inner and outer edges of the eye are either level or begin to slant upwards this shows the person is less critical.

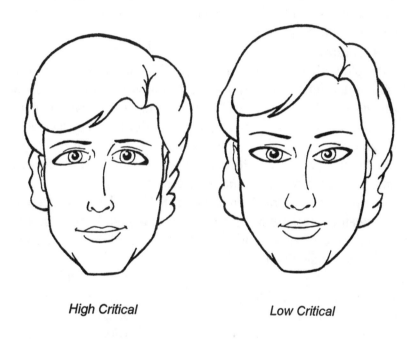

High Critical   **Low Critical**

Figure 59   Critical Perception

The first thing a critical person sees is what is wrong. It is an *automatic* thought process. For some people this is extremely annoying, however this built in attitude is invaluable in the inspection of newly manufactured jet aircraft engines on which hundreds of lives will depend. However, Criticalness does not belong in the family environment. Notice first what has been accomplished and acknowledge the person's efforts. Point out what could be improved if your advice is requested.

When the eyes slant upwards at the outer corners, these people may not to notice the flaws that are important to safety, calculations or constructing a garment They would first notice what has been achieved rather than point out what is wrong. They are non-critical people. Other traits such as Sharpness and Analyticalness would highten the low Critical person's awareness of imperfections in a product.

Trait Combinations

People with a combination of high Criticalness, high Physical Insulation (Figure 5) Low Considerateness (Figure 37) Low Tolerance (Figure 31) will be extremely critical without consideration for other peoples' feelings. Because they have low tolerance, their reaction will be shorter. These people would be very difficult to please. However, once they are aware of these traits, they can direct them more effectively.

When there is a trait combination of Critical Perception and Analyticalness (Figure 57) the effect is amplified. It can result in uncalled-for critique that may hurt the feelings of people who see no need to be digging up faults and problems. It can also make it difficult to recognize the importance of achievement rather than how well (or otherwise) the project has been done. Critical people make good critics (obviously) for books, films, art and business situations, particularly where an Analytical capability can add insight and perspective.

Directing High Critical Perception

If you are a Critical person, use criticism for on the job situations. Learn to use it in a constructive way. Remember to give equal amount of praise and acknowledgement when the job is well done. To criticize fellow workers too much may be counter-

productive and result in hard feelings.
Directing Low Critical Perception
   If you are less Critical, be more aware of the flaws on the job.
Get the advice of others who score high in this area. Double check
to make sure you have not overlooked an important fact.

JUDGEMENT VARIATION

   Judgement Variation is indicated when one eye is higher than the
other. Notice in Figure 60 both the right and left inner canthi
(inner corners of eye) of the eye. Are they level with each other,
or is one slightly higher or significantly higher? When it is
noticeably higher, people tend to have unconventional judgement.
   At times their judgement is very different from those around
them They will come up with less conventional ways of solving a
problem. To those who are more conservative, some of these
extreme approaches will be uncomfortable. The unconventional
person will approach new designs or ways to solve problems with
a different perspective, whether designing a new building, creating
an advertisement or a theatrical production.

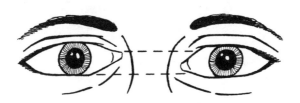

Figure 60   Judgement Variation

   When both eyes are level with each other, this person would be
more conventional and accepting of the standards set by society.
They are more predictable and conservative in their approach.

Unconventional approaches and behaviour are uncomfortable for them.

Directing Judgement Variation

If you have High Judgement Variation, then this trait can work for or against you. Use unconventional approaches when it is beneficial, otherwise be open to using conventional methods.

Directing Low Judgement Variation

If you have low Judgement Variation, be willing to adapt to less conventional ideas when appropriate.

RHETORIC

This trait is shown by the lines under the eye that go from the inner corner of the eye and continue toward the outer corner. The more lines there are and the greater length, the higher is the score. People with a strong Rhetoric trait have gift for words and love to use a large vocabulary.

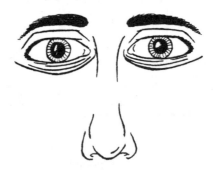

Figure 61   Rhetoric

They enjoy looking up the meanings of words and their origins and derivatives. They have a great appreciation of effective and elegant use of the language. Clumsy and incorrect word usage is offensive to them, particularly by people in high positions. When this trait is combined with Analyticalness (Figure 57) they are particularly insistent about word usage, and are quick to correct others who use grammar and words incorrectly.

Possible careers for people who score high on this trait are writing, journalism, editing, poetry and teaching.

How to Direct High Rhetoric

Listen to the content of what is being said, rather than interupt a conversation to correct that persons word usage.

How to Direct Low Rhetoric

Build up your vocabulary daily by looking up a word in the dictionary that you have heard or read that day. Then write down several different sentences using that word.

FAMOUS FACES

It's All in the Face

GÉRARD DEPARDIEU

Gérard Depardieu is a very friendly individual with an insatiable curiosity for news and information. This is shown by the roundness of the nose and flat forehead. Because he likes to start new projects, he may find himself not completing or maintaining previous ones. Ideas are constantly milling around in his head and when he decides to do something there is no stopping him. His protruding chin shows he has a tremendous amount of tenacity. His analytical eyes tell us he takes his work seriously, and asks many questions before making a decision. Balance and harmony are important to his life. He may enjoy collecting old works of art and photography, and probably has a wonderful collection of books. He will respond physically to an emergency and needs to remember to act rather than react. Competitive sports would be a good outlet for his physical and combative spirit. He is at home with nature and likes to contribute to the quality of other people's lives.

HILARY CLINTON

The width of Hilary Clinton's face shows an extremely self-confident and authoritative person. She likes to take on a challenge and enjoys the recognition that goes along with her job. Her curved eyebrow shows she is an excellent programme coordinator and has good organization skills. Her wide set eyes say she is a very tolerant person and tends to procrastinate. Her challenge is to stay focused. As a long-term planner, she will get irritated by those who move at a slower pace. Her large lower lip shows she is generous with her time and enjoys maintaining projects. She likes to entertain at home and being with people. Quick to respond, forceful and competitive, she likes to win and has good leadership qualities. Hobbies would be travel (pronounced cheek bones) reading, specialty cooking, fund raising, remodeling homes (curved forehead). She loves to be by the water or in open spaces, and prefers rounded rather than geometric designs.

MICK JAGGER

Mick Jagger's protruding lips and length above the upper lip show he is a very impulsive person with a dry sense of humor Here is a person who has the "gift of the gab". Does he ever stop talking? Mick is a very analytical person and pays close attention to detail. Notice the deep furrows between his eyebrows, he likes to get things exactly right. The inverted V-shaped eyebrow shows an appreciation of design such as in art, photography and architecture. The flat forehead implies he appreciates time on his own, which may be a challenge for him since he is constantly with people. At times he may prefer to read a book or escape to one of his favourite places. Because he is more administrative, he would prefer to oversee a project. At the same time he is very conscious of how much things cost, and he enjoys a bargain.

VANESSA REDGRAVE

It's All in the Face

Vanessa has extremely fine hair which suggests a person very sensitive to taste, touch, feelings and emotions. When her feelings are hurt, she may take a whole week to get over the incident. Her features are narrow, which shows she gains her confidence through knowledge. She may be intimidated when confronted by new and challenging situations. Vanessa has an appreciation of quality versus quantity, and she enjoys being in an elegant environment. The music needs to be softer because loud noises or people will irritate her. The thinner upper lip shows that she is a concise person, not interested in wordy discussions. She likes to come to the point quickly, but has the need to analyse situations or new products. Her sloping forehead shows a mind that works quickly, and she jumps to conclusions before all the information has been given. One eye appears higher than the other, suggesting she is less conventional in her approach. Her forehead is more rounded on her right side and the other looks more squared off. This reflects a swing mood. One part of her is the maintainer and the other side likes to start new projects. The fine hair indicates she enjoys elegant dining and soft music.

WOOPI GOLDBERG

Woopi is a very impulsive person, which may have got her into trouble at times. The sloping back forehead shows she is quick to respond to situations, whether an emergency or an ad-lib. Her high protruding cheek bones say she loves to have variety in her day, and does not enjoy repetitive situations. Her round nose shows she has a natural curiosity and enjoys being with people. She is an extremely tolerant person, but catch her at a bad time and she will be less tolerant (one eye is closer to the centre of the nose). Her high forward balance shows she loves to have an audience. Her pointed chin suggests she handles pressure well. However, there is a stubborn side to her nature.

She enjoys her home and at times may have been accused of being a pack rat. The larger lower lip shows she enjoys giving and sharing with others. If you ask her for directions, do not expect a concise answer. She will give you all the options and what to notice on the way. This is shown by her large upper lip.

ANTHONY HOPKINS

Anthony's eyelids are completely exposed, suggesting he will want to know the bottom line. At times he may appear ruthless, because of his direct approach. However, his sensitivity, which is seen with his fine hair, will help to balance the previous trait. The straight outer edge of his ear shows he has a pioneering spirit and likes to start new projects, although his curved forehead suggests there is a little of the maintainer in him. Because he likes to look at the big picture and act on it, at times he will be perceived as a moving force. His high self-confidence says he enjoys a challenge and may become quickly bored if life becomes too ordinary. He enjoys and expects recognition and appreciates the strokes that come with it. Quality comes before quantity. Soft music and fine dining are a part of his preferred lifestyle. The V-shaped eyebrows show that he likes to design and co-ordinate projects. He has a high appreciation of architecture and design. He loves to read and gather information, as shown by his rounded nose and the flatness of his forehead.

TRAITS IN ACTION

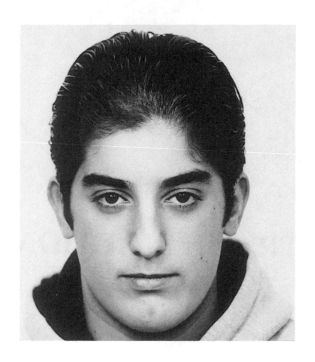

MARCUS

Eyebrows	Appreciation of balance and harmony
Hair (coarse)	Less sensitive to emotions and feelings. Enjoys the outdoors.
Thin upper lip	Concise in his delivery of speech
Nose	Looks for a bargain, value for money
Ear	Likes to collect and enjoys investments. Has high music appreciation.
Forehead	His rounded forehead indicates he enjoys his home and remodeling. He likes to maintain projects.
Width of face	High self-confidence, enjoys a challenge
Lower lip	He enjoys giving of time and presents
Careers	Forest ranger, agriculture, investments, real estate broker, hotel management.
Hobbies	Wrestling, swimming, bicycling, bowling, tai chi, camping, concerts, art,

EVELINE

Cheek bone	Adventurous, likes a variety in her day.
Nose	The bulbous nose indicates she is a very curious person. Has a love of new information.
Forehead	The squareness of forehead, indicates she enjoys starting new projects. Does not like to maintain them.
Lower Jaw	She is extremely authoritative
Width of Face	High self-confidence
Eyes	Very analytical and extremely tolerant.

Careers: Architect, couturiere, librarian, landscape architect.

Hobbies: Hiking, gardening, reading, dancing, travel, collect books, philosophical interest.

It's All in the Face

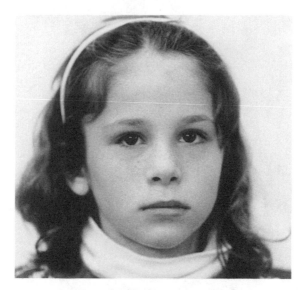

GINNY 7 year old twin

Eyes	She is an extremely tolerant person and trys to fit in too many projects. She likes the big picture. It is a challenge for her to stay focused. She has a need to analyse and ask questions.
Width of face	She enjoys a challenge. Very confident.
Ears	Has a love of music and enjoys having a collection. She likes to keep her possessions for a long time.
Thinking	Ginny is more sequential in her thought process. She needs to give herself plenty of time to study before tests.
Chin	Do not try to pressure Ginny into an activity. She works well under pressure.
Forehead	The small mounds on her forehead indicate high imagination.This is seen in both twins. Her rounded forehead indicates she likes to maintain
Careers:	Psychologist, social worker, electronic engineer, hotel management, personologist.
Hobbies:	Writing, art, singing, photography, pets, soccer, analytical games, collections, reading.

LINDSAY 7 year old twin

Ear lobes	Enjoys collecting stuffed animals. Encourage her to have savings account
High Self-Confidence	Enjoys a challenge. Good leadership potential.
Eyes	Very analytical, has a strong need to know why.
Eyebrows	The top of her eyebrow has a peak, this indicates design appreciation.
Iris	Lindsay displays warmth and magnetism. Friends will tell her their problems.
Lower lip	She has a big heart and enjoys giving of her time and presents.
Chin	Lindsay does not like being pressured into an activity. Give her the reasons why.
Career:	Teacher, electronic engineer, writer occupational therapist, composer,
Hobbies:	Poetry, have a collection, reading, writing, analytical games, singing.

The main differences between the twins is the forehead shape. This reflects the career differences. Lindsay likes to start new projects.

ALAN

Above eyebrow Pays attention to detail.

Lips Concise, uses fewer words.

Chin Enjoys verbal or physical confrontation. This can be used positively in panel debates or physical activity.

Eyes He has a swing mood in tolerance. The right eye is closer to the bridge of nose.

Eye Lid He wants to know the bottom line, rather than a lengthy analysis.

Fine Hair He is a very sensitive person. Prefers quality rather than quality. Enjoys refinement in clothing and interior design.

Eyebrows This is a very friendly person and enjoys working with people. Balance and harmony are important to him.

Careers: Hospital or college administration, hotel management, real estate broker, trainer.

Hobbies: Investments, art, photography, cooking, remodel homes, sculpture, collect stamps, coins, books.

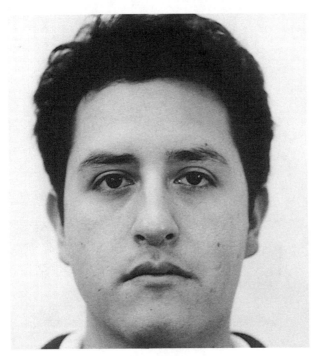

CARLOS

Eyebrows	The inverted V shape eyebrow indicates strong design abilities. He appreciates balance and harmony.
Hair	He enjoys being in the outdoor and is less sensitive to the cold climates.
Legs	Because he has very short legs, he has a physical need for exercise each day.
Nose	Carlos looks for a bargain. Enjoys investments. He is somewhat skeptical, and will question new ideas until he can form his own opinion.
Chin	Works well under pressure and can be very stubborn.
Forehead	Quick to respond in emergency situations.
Careers:	Engineer, stock broker, computer programmer, landscape architect, financing.
Hobbies:	Music, jogging, dancing, soccer, photography, art,

GREG

Nostrils	High self-reliance. This is a person who knows he can rely on his own ability to get through a situation.
Eye Lid	Very analytical and is a good problem solver.
Eye	Greg is a very tolerant person. Likes to know the big picture. May get easily distracted, the challenge is to stay focussed.
Nose	He enjoys overseeing a project. Has a good feeling for business investments.
Narrow Jaw	This face reflects less authority. However when if he wears glasses and darker clothing, he would be perceived as having higher authority.
Ears	Has a love of music and enjoys investments.
Careers:	Electronic engineer, mechanical engineer, marketing research analyst, lead workshops.
Hobbies:	Hiking, art, photography, analytical games, music, collecting stamps/coins, specialty cooking.

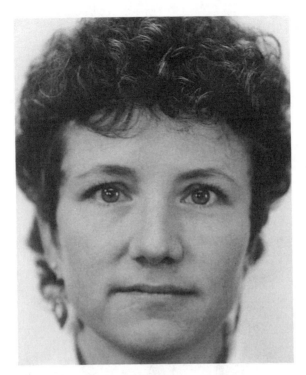

TERESA

Eyes	She is extremely tolerant and very analytical. She expresses warmth and emotion.
Eye brow	Has a good sense of design and would make a great programme director.
Width of face	Teresa likes to take on new challenges and shows good leadership qualities.
Hair fine	Because her hair is so fine, she will be very sensitive to other peoples feelings.
Jaw Line	She appears to be more authoritative and this will add to her leadership skills.
Lips	Concise and to the point with out unnecessary verbage.
Careers:	Lead workshops and seminars, training, computer programmer, occupational therapist, economist.
Hobbies:	Sing in choral group, art, photography.

It's All in the Face

DIANE

Forehead	Likes to maintain projects, remodel homes, enjoys cooking, work for an environmental cause.
Fine Hair	She appreciates quality over quantity . Her feelings get hurt very quickly.
Jaw Line	This is a very authoritative person.
Cheek bones	Enjoys travel and likes a variety in her day.
Eyes	Very expressive and emotional.
Lips	Diane is very impetuous and likes to talk. She needs to think first before she speaks and acts
Face	There is more face in front of her ear, which indicates she enjoys being on stage.
Career:	Actress, radio or tv announcer, flight attendant, playwright.
Hobbies:	Hiking, tennis, theatre, photography, travel.

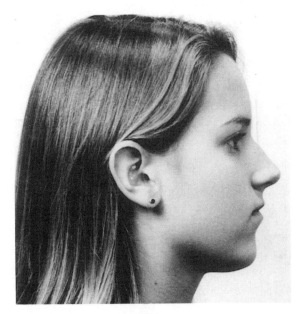

ALI

Sharp Face   She likes to ferret out information. Good
for investigations.

Nose   Likes to oversee projects. The bottom line is how
much does it cost.

Eyes   She has a swing mood on tolerance. Don't turn up
late for an appointment with her. Although rhetoric
cannot be seen in this photo, she places
high importance on word usage.

Forehead   From the side view the forehead curves outwards,
this indicates originality. Tie this in with her gift for
words, she has the potential for writing.

Nose   Ali is very open to new ideas and is a good listener.

Ears   Has a love of music.

Careers: Hospital administration, writer, teacher, hotel
receptionist, sales, accounting.

Hobbies: Swimming, bicycling, horse back riding, cooking,
writing, attend the theatre and concerts.

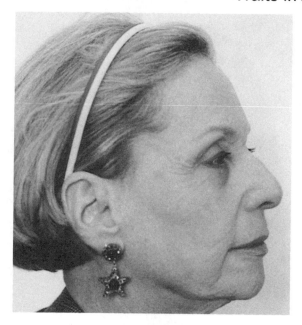

SUZANNE

Face Profile	She likes to plan long range, and is quick to respond to emergency situations. She may jump to conclusions or finish off a sentence for someone, because her mind works so quickly.
Lips	Suzanne needs to think first, or she may commit to something or say what she regrets later.
Eye brow	Very dramatic both in actions and speech
Above the lip	The length above the upper lip indicates she is known for her dry wit.
Eyes	Takes her work very seriously.
Nose	Does not accept things at face value. Loves a bargain.
Cheek bones	Needs to have a variety in her day.
Careers:	Television announcer, news commentator, sales, investments, artist.
Hobbies	Tennis, gardening, reading, travel, theatre, toastmaster, crafts.

140

LIFE'S DAILY EXPERIENCES

- **Personal Development**
- **10 Acre Principle**
- **Marriage**
- **Childhood Development**
- **Career Choices**
- **Sales**
- **Business**
- **Jury Selection**

APPLICATION TO LIFE'S DAILY EXPERIENCES

Personal Development and Awareness

Once a personology consultation has been completed, and the results set out on a chart, it gives the recipient an overview of themselves that is not judgmental. It is a blueprint that allows them to look at each part of themselves objectively without feeling threatened or being diagnosed as perfect or imperfect. It gives an insight into the areas that may need more conscious awareness of the positive or negative aspects, as perceived by themselves and others.

People can be intimidating, without intending to be, because of a combination of high Self-Confidence, Authoritativeness and Objectiveness. Knowing that this is a part of their genetic makeup, they have a choice of modifying or using these traits to their advantage.   Recognizing the need to modify their perceived intimidation will help them to communicate with others who score low in these traits.

Imagine a child whose traits are completely opposite to the parents' traits. This could present a problem and inhibit the child's personal growth and development. As some of you read this, I am sure you can relate to situations where you were neither encouraged nor supported in pursuing activities that interested you. Or there may have been times when you were struggling through school and your grades did not meet your parent's expectations. Worse still, you were considered to have a learning problem or you were not too bright. This situation could apply to any phase in a person's life if the environment, whether personal or business, is non supportive.

A recent newspaper article reported that a partition was placed around the desk of a disruptive child to isolate him from the rest of the class. His photograph showed him to be an extremely Tolerant (wide eye spacing) young man. There is a multitude of ideas constantly going around in his head, and he loves attention. There were other traits contributing to his disruptive activities. Once they are identified, both the teacher and the parents could handle the problem more constructively.

Personology gives us the opportunity to take a good look at ourselves and help us to understand others. It is not about answering a set of questions to decide which category you fall into. This study is different. We are looking at our genetic structure that reflects our unique qualities and abilities. It puts us in touch with who we are, helping us to find answers within, and to live a more balanced and harmonious life.

The Ten-Acre Principle

This is an area that plays an important role in personal relationships and marriage. The ten-acre principle defines the space around two people when they interact. Each person has their own ten-acre private domain, which should not be intruded upon by the other unless invited. Then there is another ten acres which are shared by both sides. In-laws are often guilty of invading the private ten-acres of their sons and daughters. For example they visit their son and immediately take over and change arrangements in the home; or they purchase items for the daughter-in-law to use without asking her if she needs them. Re-organizing the cupboards or refrigerator may be done with good intentions. However, this steps into the other person's ten acres, and may cause bad feelings. In-laws are there, hopefully, to play a supportive role, and help out and give advice only when requested.

Young children also need their own private area, whether it is their own room or a special place to keep their treasures. People who are highly Considerate, Forceful and Ministrative may be inclined to "butt in" when they may not be welcome, and interfere in other people's affairs. The ten-acre principle applies to both personal and business relationships.

Marriage

An important ingredient for a successful marriage or personal relationship is the understanding and respect of both oneself and the other person. When two people are spending a good part of their life together, it is important for them to understand each other's traits *and* how they interact together. Do they clash or are they similar? Consider for example fine hair versus coarse hair. One person may prefer more elegance, soft music, quality rather than quantity and a more gentle approach to the relationship. The person with coarse hair may enjoy more of everything, whether it is sound, food, quantity versus quality or their approach to intimate situations. There may be even greater differences, such as one person likes to be constantly active, while the other person enjoys just staying at home. When people have a combination of Analyticalness, high Self-Confidence, Critical Perception and coarse hair, they appear to put down or constantly find fault with other members of the family or co-workers. This may not be their intent, but just the traits in action. When people with these traits become aware of the negative communication, they can consciously choose to override this tendency. Personology heightens the awareness of oneself and others, whether spouse, child or co-worker. It helps to eliminate misunderstanding and create a supportive environment.

Opposites usually attract each other. Before making the commitment of living together, couples should consider whether contrasting traits could cause problems. If so, can both parties come to an understanding of each other's needs and how to express them? Are they differences that each can live with? Each person in the marriage or relationship needs to work on their own traits, and consider how to express their feelings to the other person. It is not about "Well if he or she doesn't work on their traits then I won't." Each of us needs to set the example and be willing to grow in the relationship. Personology plays an important role in identifying each person's genetic traits and how they interact with one another. There should be at least five major trait areas that are similar between two people in a relationship. Although this does not guarantee a life time relationship, it will certainly help the friendship be more compatible. Having a personology chart made helps to avoid conflicts and misunderstanding between spouses and family members. During a 1960 survey, couples who had a personology consultation revealed that 92% of the cases it helped to preserve the marriage.

Childhood Development

Knowledge of your children's traits significantly contributes to the understanding and handling of different situations, whether in communication or when discipline is needed. It helps in discovering what their interests are, their need for physical activity, and the kinds of sports and hobbies they would enjoy.

A young boy who scored high on Acquisitiveness (enjoying collecting or investments) was asked what his hobbies were. It was not surprising to learn that he had a large rock collection that he had been gathering for many years. As parents recognizing this trait in a child, they would encourage and support this activity.

In handling the child with high Ego and coarse hair, they would teach him to be aware of others needs. For the child who has low Self-Confidence, encourage and acknowledge his achievements. When children are struggling with subjects they do not understand, take them through each step so that they really grasp all there is to know before going to the next level.

Knowing your children's innate abilities and talents, how they communicate, and how they feel emotionally and physically, how they process information, these all assist a parent through the many stages of development. Currently this approach is being used in private schools with great success. The children get a better understanding of themselves and how to communicate with others. It also helps the teachers when they have the students' personology charts available, so that they can direct them in constructive ways.

Time for Change

I was employed 15 years by a major transportation company as a safety engineer, and had advanced as far as I could go. It was time to make a change. After a personology consultation, a sales career was suggested. I accepted an appointment as a State Farm agent. That was 30 years ago. I am still amazed at how accurate the chart was, it hit the nail on the head for me. Thanks Personology. Omar Sharp, State Farm, CA

Career Choices

Within the last few years there has been a dramatic increase in the number of people facing career change. With the downsizing of companies and the reorganizations, many people are considering other job possibilities. They are asking themselves what really motivates them, and what other options do they have that will give them greater job satisfaction. How many college students actually know what their major will be? Most change their major as many as three times, and only 30% of post graduate students stay with their original major. Although they may have gone through one of the testing programmes (this works for some students), something still doesn't feel quite right. They find themselves in the dilemma of still not knowing which direction to take their career.

Mentioned earlier in the book, personology yields similar results to multiple-choice testing such as Meyers Briggs. Major differences are that no questions are asked, and, for each career suggested, the percentage of matching traits is given. A personology consultation can reduce trial and error and establish information that helps in finding the career path that best reflects each person's innate abilities. The consultation often validates what has already been considered and gives "permission" to move forward on those ideas with more confidence, knowing that this time they are on the right track. Over a hundred measurements are taken during a personology consultation. Once these have been charted, both the high and low pole scores are considered when matching the traits for vocational guidance. The following are some examples of career matching once a person has had their chart made. If a person's traits matched all of the following areas they would enjoy a career as an engineer: Interest in Information, Analytical, Multiplicity of Ideas, Imagination, Sound Appreciation, Structural Appreciation and high Comprehension. For a real estate broker the traits would need to be high on: Interest in Information, Interest in People, Administrative, Forcefulness, Objective Thinking, Acquisitive, Nose for News and Humor. Therapists would need high people skills, Hand and Foot Dexterity, Conservation, Tolerance, Considerateness, Estheticness and low to medium Physical Insulation.

When you choose a career, this is a massive investment of time and money. This is true whether you are a new college student, re-entering the job market or looking for a career change. It makes sense to seek advice and confirmation on a career direction that best reflects one's innate abilities. After all we are going to spend many years working, why not avoid the trial and error? So many people are finding themselves imprisoned in jobs they really do not enjoy. Because the job offers security, there is a reluctance to consider other possibilities. Living a life of compromise has no lasting satisfaction. It may even create a negative environment that overflows into the home, affecting the lives of those around you. Women for most part generally ask themselves that soul-searching question at an earlier age, whereas men may have seldom allowed themselves the luxury of considering a change. When they are in a secure position in the company, financial demands cause them to tolerate the lack of satisfaction, rather than risk pursuing a new career that would bring them greater personal reward.

A situation that comes to mind is a salesman who, although successful at his job, was not a happy person. Something was throwing his life out of balance, and as a result he sought alcohol to escape the frustration, to the point where it was affecting his job. It was recommended that a personology chart would help him to get a better understanding of what was happening. What he discovered was that he was in the wrong type of job. The comment made by the personologist, who was unaware of the drinking problem, was that his present job was enough to send him to drink. This man changed his job and experienced a significant impact on his life. What he discovered was that although of slender build, he was more suited to operating heavy road equipment. He took a job in a construction company, which he really enjoyed, and desire for alcohol was no longer a problem.

Sales

Knowing who your prospect is in thirty seconds could make all the difference when meeting for the first time. Knowledge of your customer's traits helps you to recognize the style of presentation and communication that will be most effective. In today's competitive market, we need as many tools as possible to be successful. Having read this book, you will better understand how and why your customer acts or reacts. For example, when your client is more Discriminating, be more formal and avoid using first names (unless this has already been established). Allow them more time and space during the negotiations and do not press for a decision, particularly if they also score high on Automatic Resistance. If the client has high Self-Confidence and high Tolerance, use bigger gestures, prove you know your subject well, respond with assurance, and give them the big picture. When you are dealing with people who are more Subjective, understand they need to process new information sequentially. Do not jump ahead or try to hurry them before they have really understood each point. The following is a profile of a customer you are meeting for the first time: Fine hair, high in Conservation, Analytical, low Self-Confidence, Concise, Automatic Resistance, Administrative, Discrimination and Interest in Information (as shown by a flat forehead rather than rounded). This person is looking for a quality product/service that will serve more than one purpose. The price will be important and they will want to know that they are getting good value for their money. The customer will ask to see other products that are similar, and ask what is the reliability, and what are they getting for the higher price. They will need a full explanation of the different features and their benefits. They are not familiar with the brand name and would wonder how easy it would be for them to use the product, and whether it is dependable. Is there information included in the package on how to use the product? The last part deals with reassurance. If this is not addressed then they may avoid buying from lack of confidence in the reliability and sincerity of the sales agent. A sale can also be lost if the customers feel pressured into buying. When they are shopping for a service, take the time to ask them what they are specifically looking for. Then respond to them based on how this fits their traits.

Building an Effective Sales Team
No part of building a sales organization is more important than the selection of new recruits. Personology was the significant contributor for developing a good team. Each recruit was given a copy of their personology chart with a detailed explanation of their strengths and weaknesses. This helped them utilize their strengths and add to their success in sales. Don Wilson, CLU

It's All in the Face

Business

Hiring the right person for the job makes all the difference in the world. How many people are truly happy in their jobs? A major problem in small restaurants is that they often hire the wrong person for the job. The training is often insufficient to ensure that the employee turns out a good product, and learns customer skills. People are moved into management positions without adequate explanation of their new job, and how to communicate with the other employees. Therefore there is a high turnover of staff and unpleasant working conditions due to communication problems between employees and their bosses. This is always counter-productive. The boss may be highly critical, analytical and forceful, and have low tolerance. The manager may get impatient when a job does not move at the pace he demands, or other employees do not live up to his own standards and expectations. All this person will notice is what has not been done, rather than the progress made. This would be a very difficult person to please. However once they are made aware of their own traits they can choose to modify their approach and communicate more productively.

If all prospective employees were screened this way, the right person would be hired more often. Productivity would go up, and the general morale and communication within the organization would be improved.

Many companies use methods to improve communication, in which groups of employees observe each other's behaviour and select categories for it such as expressive-amiable, analytical-driver, etc. However with personology, even more information can be obtained within just minutes, without verbal information or group interaction.

Most accomplishments in business are the result of successful team work by people of diverse personalities and interests. Here accurate and timely communication is crucially important. However some problems of communication is the miscommunication that happens where people receive the information entirely differently from what was intended.

This is where personology plays a key role in business. It helps each person to develop a conscious awareness, not only of themselves but also of the people they interact with. This creates a higher level of communication and understanding that immediately raises the morale of the organization. Personology shows how and why people communicate and processes information, and the way they feel and respond emotionally in any given situation. It helps us to build an effective team.

Jury Selection

There are many strong indicators in the face which reflect the way an individual will act or react. Personology will help by identifying these tendencies before the trial begins. This way the attorney can avoid people they do not want on the jury, and better predict the favorable responses of those selected. They will then be able to direct the questioning and eye contact in a way that will support a positive outcome for the case.

Dr. Bruce Vaughan, a specialist in trial psychology, is considered to be among the foremost trial consultants in the country. He states that personology significantly contributed to the success of the 80% cases won. To determine who you want on the jury, create an ideal profile and a negative profile. This will assist you in getting a clear picture of the panel that would best serve your case, and of the candidates you do not want on the jury. Once these profiles have been determined, personology will then help in selecting the people who best fit the ideal profile. It gives the attorney insight about jurors that would not otherwise be available. This insight can be used throughout the trial for directing or making eye contact with a juror. When the attorney wishes to emphasize a point, an immediate reaction will be noticed.

If you are representing the plaintiff, there are certain people who will not help your case. When stress is indicated by the white of the eye being exposed under the iris, the person may be going through strong personal problems that would distract from the trial issues. Skeptical and Critical jurors are harder to convince, and might well cause a delay in the process or result in a hung jury. The following are some examples of traits which can be matched with the best-case and worst-case jury profiles.

The person with an Administrative nose is tight on money. If the case involves a dollar settlement, and there are several people on the jury with this trait, then an attorney would need to increase the sum to get a settlement closer to the acceptable compensation. In contrast a juror with a larger lower lip, indicating generosity, would be favorable to the plaintiff and would be inclined to award a larger sum.

Low Tolerance people like to live by the rules and it is doubtful that anything that is said will change their beliefs. In contrast, an Analytical person is concerned with facts and figures, and will feel a need to have all the information in place before making a decision.

GLOSSARY OF TERMS

ACQUISITIVENESS	The need to aquire posssions
ADVENTUROUSNESS	Inclination towards change and excitement
ADMINISTRATIVE	A natural tendency to administrate/oversee
AFFABLE	Enjoys meeting people. Very approachable
ANLYTICAL	How much a person analyses
AUTHORITATIVENESS	Naturally authoritative
AUTOMATIC-GIVING	Automatic giving with no strings attached
BALANCE,BACKWARD	Relates to what has happened and the present
BALANCE,FORWARD	Think in terms of the future rather than historical
CONCISENESS	Brevity of expression
CONSERVATION	To maintain and look after
CONSERVATISM	A more conservative approach to high risk
CONSTRUCTION	Enjoys starting new projects, does not like to maintain
CREDULITY	To be open to new ideas

It's All in the Face

CRITICAL-PERCEPTION — An awareness of variation from the rule

DETAIL CONCERN — The habitual focus on detail

DISCRIMINATIVE — To be selective

DRAMATIC-APPRECIATION — Exaggerated communication and action

DRY WIT — Dry sense of humor

ESTHETIC-APPRECIATION — An appreciation of balance and harmony

EXACTINGNESS — The need to have something exactly right

FOOT-DEXTERITY — The need to sit or stand

GROWING TREND — Interest in all aspects of personal growth and horticulture

HAND-DEXTERITY — Co-ordination of the hands

IDEALIZING-TREND — A conception how things should be. Realistic or idealistic

IMPULSIVENESS — To respond instinctively both verbally and physically

INNATE-SELF-CONFIDENCE — Built in self-confidence

INSTINCTIVE-SELF-RELIANCE — The ability to rely on one's self in challenging situations

JUDGEMENT-VARIATION — An unconventional approach

MENTAL-MOTIVE — Amount of Mental activity

METHODICALNESS	The habitual reliance on methodical routine
MINISTRATIVE	To spontaneously serve and look after
MOOD SWINGS	To suddenly switch to a different mood without any warning
OBJECTIVE-THINKING	The timing of the mental process
OPTIMISM	Habitual attitude of thinking positive
PHILOSOPHICAL-TREND	Strong philosophical interests
PHYSICAL-INSULATION	The insulation to external circumstances
PHYSICAL-MAGNETISM	The amount of warmth in a persons eyes
PHYSICAL-MOTIVE	A tendency to react physically
PHYSICALNESS	Physical stamina
PIONEER	To explore new concepts and new territory
RHETORIC	An appreciation of correct word usage
SERIOUS-MINDEDNESS	Takes life too seriously
SHARPNESS	Exremely aware of what is happening
SOUND-APPRECIATION	A high appreciation of music

It's All in the Face

PRIDE IN PERSONAL APPEARANCE	Takes things personally
TAKES-CHANCES	Risk taker
TOLERANCE	Timing of emotional action to what is seen or sensed
VERBOSENESS	The need to embelish a conversation

INDEX

It's All in the Face

APPENDIX

Classes, Workshops and Services

Individual Charts for Career Guidance Whether you are a college student, re-entering the work force or in mid-life career change, personology charts will help to eliminate confusion and assist you in making important career decisions.

Personal Development and Communication
Many people have experienced the frustration of never understanding who they really are. They have experienced a lack of identity or validation growing up within the family structure or in their personal and business lives. Personology gives each person a unique insight of themselves and how they can create a sense of balance and harmony into all aspects of their lives.

Marriage Guidance A personology consultation clearly explains the differences in personality traits and the possible reasons for conflict in marriage. Many couples have reconsidered separation after having their charts made and have subsequently stayed together.

Seminars and Workshops Would you like to increase your sales, improve employee relationships and communications? We offer half or whole day workshops which are held either on-site or at locations which are more relaxing.

Personnel Screening for Companies We provide assistance in selecting the most suitable people for the job.

Personology as a Profession Are you interested in becoming a certified personologist? Correspondence courses are available.

Please contact us at the address given below.

Personal Profile by Mail Send three photographs (3x5 inches, full face and both side profiles with the ear exposed) plus at least ten strands of hair (taped to a card) from each side just above the ear. Mark which side they come from. $35.00 per person.

Sponsoring Group Consultation These services are offered throughout the United States, Europe. To set up group consultations in your area, please contact the International Centre for Personology.

Additional Copies of *It's All in the Face* may be purchased directly from the address below.

Call or write to: Naomi R. Tickle
                International Centre for Personology
                P.O. Box 4439, Mountain View
                CA 94040   USA
                (415) 965-9540 Fax (415) 965-9839

BIBLIOGRAPHY

Whiteside, Robert L., *This is Personology,* The Interstate Personology College Press, San Francisco, 1962

Whiteside, Robert L., *Personology, The Dynamics of Success,* Frederick Fell, Inc. New York, 1969

Whiteside, Robert L., *Face Language II*, Frederick Fell Publishers, Inc. Hollywood, Florida, 1988

Tao, Li, *How to Read Faces*, Hamlyn, Great Britain, 1989

It's All in the Face

ORDER FORM

* Fax orders: (415) 965-9839
* Telephone orders: call (415) 965-9540. Have your VISA or MasterCard ready
* Postal orders: Make checks payable to: Naomi Tickle, P.O. Box 4439, Mountain View, CA 94040 USA
  Tel: (415) 965-9540

* Please send *It's All in the Face* to:

Company Name:_____

Name:_____

Address:_____

City:_____State:_____Zip:_____

Telephone:(_____)_____

Sales Tax: Please add 8% for orders shipped to California
Shipping: Book rate: $2.00 for the first book and 75 cents for each additional book (Surface shipping may take three to four weeks)
Air Mail: $3.50 per book.

Payment:
* Check
* Credit card: VISA   MasterCard
  Card number:_____Exp. date:___

Name on card: _____

It's All in the Face

ORDER FORM

* Fax orders: (415) 965-9839
* Telephone orders: call (415) 965-9540. Have your VISA or MasterCard ready
* Postal orders: Make checks payable to: Naomi Tickle, P.O. Box 4439, Mountain View, CA 94040   USA
  Tel: (415) 965-9540

* Please send *It's All in the Face* to:

Company Name:_____

Name:_____

Address:_____

City:_____State:_____Zip:_____

Telephone:(_____)_____

Sales Tax: Please add 8% for orders shipped to California
Shipping: Book rate: $2.00 for the first book and 75 cents for each additional book (Surface shipping may take three to four weeks)
Air Mail: $3.50 per book.

Payment:
* Check
* Credit card: VISA   MasterCard
  Card number:_____Exp. date:___

Name on card: _____